Edward Bulwer

Kenelm Chillingly

His adventures and opinions

Edward Bulwer

Kenelm Chillingly
His adventures and opinions

ISBN/EAN: 9783741164934

Manufactured in Europe, USA, Canada, Australia, Japa

Cover: Foto ©Andreas Hilbeck / pixelio.de

Manufactured and distributed by brebook publishing software (www.brebook.com)

Edward Bulwer

Kenelm Chillingly

COLLECTION
OF
BRITISH AUTHORS

TAUCHNITZ EDITION.

VOL. 1311.

KENELM CHILLINGLY
By EDWARD BULWER, LORD LYTTON.

IN FOUR VOLUMES.
VOL. IV.

KENELM CHILLINGLY

HIS

ADVENTURES AND OPINIONS

BY

EDWARD BULWER, LORD LYTTON.

COPYRIGHT EDITION.

IN FOUR VOLUMES.
VOL. IV.

LEIPZIG
BERNHARD TAUCHNITZ
1873.

KENELM CHILLINGLY.

BOOK VI. *(Continued.)*

CHAPTER XV.

KENELM did indeed find a huge pile of letters and notes on reaching his forsaken apartment in Mayfair—many of them merely invitations for days long past, none of them of interest except two from Sir Peter, three from his mother, and one from Tom Bowles.

Sir Peter's were short. In the first he gently scolded Kenelm for going away without communicating any address; and stated the acquaintance he had formed with Gordon, the favourable impression that young gentleman had made on him, the transfer of the £20,000, and the invitation given to Gordon, the Traverses, and Lady Glenalvon. The second, dated much later, noted the arrival of his invited guests, dwelt with warmth unusual to Sir Peter on the attractions of Cecilia, and took occasion to refer, not the less emphatically because as it were incidentally, to the sacred promise which Kenelm had given him never to propose to a young lady until the case had been submitted to the examination and received the consent of Sir Peter. "Come to Exmundham, and if I do not give my consent to propose to Cecilia Travers, hold me a tyrant and rebel."

Lady Chillingly's letters were much longer. They dwelt more complainingly on his persistence in eccentric habits—so exceedingly unlike other people, quitting London at the very height of the season, going without even a servant nobody knew where—she did not wish to wound his feelings; but still those were not the ways natural to a young gentleman of station. If he had no respect for himself he ought to have some consideration for his parents, especially his poor mother. She then proceeded to comment on the elegant manners of Leopold Travers, and the good sense and pleasant conversation of Chillingly

Gordon, a young man of whom any mother might be proud. From that subject she diverged to mildly querulous references to family matters. Parson John had expressed himself very rudely to Mr. Chillingly Gordon upon some book by a foreigner—Comte, or Count, or some such name—in which, so far as she could pretend to judge, Mr. Gordon had uttered some very benevolent sentiments about humanity, which, in the most insolent manner, Parson John had denounced as an attack on religion. But really Parson John was too High Church for her. Having thus disposed of Parson John, she indulged some lady-like wailings on the singular costume of the three Miss Chillinglys. They had been asked by Sir Peter, unknown to her—so like him—to meet their guests; to meet Lady Glenalvon and Miss Travers, whose dress was so perfect (here she described their dress)—and they came in pea-green with pelerines of mock blonde, and Miss Sally with corkscrew ringlets and a wreath of jessamine, "which no girl after eighteen would venture to wear."

"But, my dear," added her ladyship, "your poor father's family are certainly great oddities. I have more to put up with than any one knows. I do my best to carry it off. I know my duties, and will do them."

Family grievances thus duly recorded and lamented, Lady Chillingly returned to her guests.

Evidently unconscious of her husband's designs on Cecilia, she dismissed her briefly: "A very handsome young lady, though rather too blonde for her taste, and certainly with an air *distingué*." Lastly, she enlarged on the extreme pleasure she felt on meeting again *the* friend of her youth, Lady Glenalvon.

"Not at all spoilt by the education of the great world, which, alas! obedient to the duties of wife and mother, however little my sacrifices are appreciated, I have long since relinquished. Lady Glenalvon suggests turning that hideous old moat into a fernery—a great improvement. Of course your poor father makes objections."

Tom's letter was written on blackedged paper, and ran thus:—

"Dear Sir,—Since I had the honour to see you in London I have had a sad loss—my poor uncle is no more. He died very suddenly after a hearty supper. One doctor says it was apoplexy, another valvular disease of the heart. He has left me his heir, after providing for his sister— no one had an idea that he had saved so much money. I am quite a rich man now. And I shall leave the veterinary business, which of late— since I took to reading, as you kindly advised— is not much to my liking. The principal corn-merchant here has offered to take me into partnership; and, from what I can see, it will be a very good thing, and a great rise in life. But, sir, I can't settle to it at present—I can't settle, as I would wish, to anything. I know you will not laugh at me when I say I have a strange longing to travel for awhile. I have been reading books of travels, and they get into my head more than any other books. But I don't think I could leave the country with a contented heart, till I have had just another look at you know whom—just to see her and know she is happy. I am sure I could shake hands with Will, and kiss her little one without a wrong thought. What do you say to that, dear sir? You promised to write to me about Her. But I have not heard from you. Susy, the little girl with the flowerball, has had a loss too—the poor old man she lived with died within a few days of my dear uncle's decease. Mother moved here, as I think you know, when the forge at Graveleigh was sold; and she is going to take Susy to live with her. She is quite fond of Susy. Pray let me hear from you soon, and do, dear sir, give me your advice about travelling—and about Her. You see I should like Her to think of me more kindly when I am in distant parts.

"I remain, dear sir,
"Your grateful servant,
"T. Bowles.

"P.S.—Miss Travers has sent me Will's last remittance. There is very little owed me now; so they must be thriving. I hope She is not overworked."

On returning by the train that evening Kenelm went to the house of Will Somers. The shop was already closed, but he was admitted by a trusty servant-maid to the parlour, where he found them all at supper, except indeed the baby, who had long since retired to the cradle, and the cradle had been removed upstairs. Will and Jessie were very proud when Kenelm invited himself to share their repast, which, though simple, was by no means a bad one. When the meal was over and the supper things removed, Kenelm drew his chair near to the glass door which led into a little garden very neatly kept —for it was Will's pride to attend to it—before he sat down to his more professional work. The door was open, and admitted the coolness of the starlit air and the fragrance of the sleeping flowers.

"You have a pleasant home here, Mrs. Somers."

"We have, indeed, and know how to bless him we owe it to."

"I am rejoiced to think that. How often when God designs a special kindness to us He puts the kindness into the heart of a fellow-man—perhaps the last fellow-man we should have thought of; but in blessing him we thank God who inspired him. Now, my dear friends, I know that you all three suspect me of being the agent whom God chose for His benefits. You fancy that it was from me came the loan which enabled you to leave Graveleigh and settle here. You are mistaken—you look incredulous."

"It could not be the Squire," exclaimed Jessie. "Miss Travers assured me that it was neither he nor herself. Oh, it must be you, sir. I beg pardon, but who else could it be?"

"Your husband shall guess. Suppose, Will, that you had behaved ill to some one who was nevertheless dear to you, and on thinking over it afterwards felt very sorry and much ashamed of yourself, and suppose that later you had the opportunity and the power to render a service to that person, do you think you would do it?"

"I should be a bad man if I did not."

"Bravo! And supposing that when the person you thus served came to know it was you who rendered the service, he did not feel thankful, he did not think it handsome of you, thus to repair any little harm he might have done you before, but became churlish, and sore, and cross-grained, and with a wretched false pride said that because he had offended you once he resented your taking the liberty of befriending him now, would not you think that person an ungrateful fellow—ungrateful not only to you his fellow-man—that is of less moment—but ungrateful to the God who put it into your heart to be His human agent in the benefit received?"

"Well, sir, yes, certainly," said Will, with all the superior refinement of his intellect to that of Jessie, unaware of what Kenelm was driving at; while Jessie, pressing her hands tightly together, turning pale, and with a frightened hurried glance towards Will's face, answered impulsively:

"Oh, Mr. Chillingly, I hope you are not thinking, not speaking of Mr. Bowles?"

"Whom else should I think, or speak of?"

Will rose nervously from his chair, all his features writhing.

"Sir, sir, this is a bitter blow—very bitter, very."

Jessie rushed to Will, flung her arms round him, and sobbed.

Kenelm turned quietly to old Mrs. Somers, who had suspended the work on which since supper she had been employed, knitting socks for the baby,

"My dear Mrs. Somers, what is the good of being a grandmother and knitting socks for baby grandchildren, if you cannot assure those silly children of yours that they are too happy in each other to harbour any resentment against a man who would have parted them, and now repents?"

Somewhat to Kenelm's admiration, I dare not say surprise, old Mrs. Somers, thus appealed to, rose from her seat, and, with a dignity of thought or of feeling no one could have anticipated from the quiet peasant woman, approached the wedded pair, lifted Jessie's face with one hand, laid the other on Will's head, and said, "If you don't long to see Mr. Bowles again and say 'the Lord bless you, sir!' you don't deserve the Lord's blessing upon you." Therewith she went back to her seat, and resumed her knitting.

"Thank Heaven, we have paid back the best part of the loan," said Will, in very agitated tones, "and I think, with a little pinching, Jessie, and with selling off some of the stock, we might pay the rest; and then"—and then he turned to Kenelm—"and then, sir, we will" (here a gulp) "thank Mr. Bowles."

"This don't satisfy me at all, Will," answered Kenelm; "and since I helped to bring you two together, I claim the right to say I would never have done so could I have guessed you could have trusted your wife so little as to allow a remembrance of Mr. Bowles to be a thought of pain. You did not feel humiliated when you imagined that it was to me you owed some moneys which you have been honestly paying off. Well, then, I will lend you whatever trifle remains to discharge your whole debts to Mr. Bowles, so that you may sooner be able to say to him, 'Thank you.' But between you and me,

Will, I think you will be a finer fellow and a manlier fellow if you decline to borrow that trifle of me; if you feel you would rather say 'Thank you' to Mr. Bowles, without the silly notion that when you have paid him his money you owe him nothing for his kindness."

Will looked away, irresolutely. Kenelm went on: "I have received a letter from Mr. Bowles to-day. He has come into a fortune, and thinks of going abroad for a time; but before he goes, he says he should like to shake hands with Will, and be assured by Jessie that all his old rudeness is forgiven. He had no notion that I should blab about the loan; he wished that to remain always a secret. But between friends there need be no secrets. What say you, Will? As head of this household, shall Mr. Bowles be welcomed here as a friend or not?"

"Kindly welcome," said old Mrs. Somers, looking up from the socks.

"Sir," said Will, with sudden energy, "look here; you have never been in love, I dare say. If you had, you would not be so hard on me.

Mr. Bowles was in love with my wife there. Mr. Bowles is a very fine man, and I am a cripple."

"Oh, Will! Will!" cried Jessie.

"But I trust my wife with my whole heart and soul; and, now that the first pang is over, Mr. Bowles shall be, as mother says, kindly welcome —heartily welcome."

"Shake hands. Now you speak like a man, Will. I hope to bring Bowles here to supper before many days are over."

And that night Kenelm wrote to Mr. Bowles:

"My dear Tom,—Come and spend a few days with me at Cromwell Lodge, Moleswick. Mr. and Mrs. Somers wish much to see and to thank you. I could not remain for ever degraded in order to gratify your whim. They would have it that I bought their shop, &c., and I was forced in self-defence to say who it was. More on this and on travels when you come.

"Your true friend,

"K. C."

CHAPTER XVI.

Mrs. Cameron was seated alone in her pretty drawing-room, with a book lying open, but unheeded, on her lap. She was looking away from its pages, seemingly into the garden without, but rather into empty space.

To a very acute and practised observer, there was in her countenance an expression which baffled the common eye.

To the common eye it was simply vacant; the expression of a quiet, humdrum woman, who might have been thinking of some quiet humdrum household detail—found that too much for her, and was now not thinking at all.

But to the true observer, there were in that face indications of a troubled past, still haunted with ghosts never to be laid at rest; indications too of a character in herself that had undergone some revolutionary change; it had not always been the character of a woman quiet and humdrum. The delicate outlines of the lip and nostril evinced sensibility, and the deep and downward curve of it bespoke habitual sadness. The softness of the look into space did not tell of a vacant mind, but rather of a mind subdued and over-burthened by the weight of a secret sorrow. There was also about her whole presence, in the very quiet which made her prevalent external characteristic, the evidence of manners formed in a high-bred society—the society in which quiet is connected with dignity and grace. The poor understood this better than her rich acquaintances at Moleswick, when they said, "Mrs. Cameron was every inch a lady." To judge by her features she must once have been pretty, not a showy prettiness, but decidedly pretty. Now, as the features were small, all prettiness had faded away in cold grey colourings, and a sort of tamed and slumbering timidity of aspect. She was not only not demonstrative, but must have imposed on herself as a duty the suppression of demonstration. Who could look at the formation of those lips, and not see that they belonged to the nervous, quick, demonstrative temperament? And yet, observing her again more closely, that suppression of the constitutional tendency to candid betrayal of emotion, would the more enlist your curiosity or interest; because, if physiognomy and phrenology have any truth in them, there was little strength in her character. In the womanly yieldingness of the short curved upper lip, the pleading timidity of the *regard*, the disproportionate but elegant slenderness of the head between the ear and the neck, there were the tokens of one who cannot resist the will, perhaps the whim, of another whom she either loves or trusts.

The book open on her lap is a serious book on the doctrine of grace, written by a popular clergyman of what is termed "the Low Church." She seldom read any but serious books, except where such care as she gave to Lily's education compelled her to read 'Outlines of History and Geography,' or the elementary French books used in seminaries for young ladies. Yet if any one had decoyed Mrs. Cameron into familiar conversation, he would have discovered that she must early have received the education given to young ladies of station. She could speak and write French and Italian as a native. She had read, and still remembered, such classic authors in either language as are conceded to the use of pupils, by the well-regulated taste of orthodox governesses. She had a knowledge of botany, such as botany was taught twenty years ago. I am not sure that, if her memory had been fairly aroused, she might not have come out strong in divinity and political economy, as expounded by the popular manuals of Mrs. Marcet. In short, you could see in her a thoroughbred English lady, who had been taught in a generation before Lily's, and immeasurably superior in culture to the ordinary run of English young ladies taught nowadays. So, in what after all are very minor accomplishments—now made major accomplishments—such as music, it was impossible that a connoisseur should hear her play on the piano without remarking, "That woman has had the best masters of her time." She could only play pieces that belonged to her generation. She had learned nothing since. In short, the whole intellectual culture had come to a dead stop long years ago, perhaps before Lily was born.

Now, while she is gazing into space, Mrs. Braefield is announced. Mrs. Cameron does not start from reverie. She never starts. But she makes a weary movement of annoyance, resettles herself, and lays the serious book on the sofa table. Elsie enters, young, radiant, dressed in all the perfection of the fashion, that is, as ungracefully as in the eyes of an artist any gentlewoman can be; but rich merchants who are proud of their wives so insist, and their wives, in that respect, submissively obey them.

The ladies interchange customary salutations, enter into the customary preliminaries of talk, and, after a pause, Elsie begins in earnest.

"But shan't I see Lily? Where is she?"

"I fear she is gone into the town. A poor little boy, who did our errands, has met with an accident—fallen from a cherry-tree."

"Which he was robbing?"

"Probably."

"And Lily has gone to lecture him?"

"I don't know as to that; but he is much hurt, and Lily has gone to see what is the matter with him."

Mrs. Braefield, in her frank outspoken way:

"I don't take much to girls of Lily's age in general, though I am passionately fond of children. You know how I do take to Lily; perhaps, because she is so like a child. But she must be an anxious charge to you."

Mrs. Cameron replied by an anxious "No. She is still a child, a very good one; why should I be anxious?"

Mrs. Braefield, impulsively:

"Why, your child must now be eighteen."

Mrs. Cameron:

"Eighteen—is it possible! How time flies! though in a life so monotonous as mine, time does not seem to fly, it slips on like the lapse of water. Let me think—eighteen? No, she is but seventeen—seventeen last May."

Mrs. Braefield: "Seventeen! A very anxious

age for a girl; an age in which dolls cease and lovers begin."

Mrs. Cameron, not so languidly, but still quietly:

"Lily never cared much for dolls—never much for lifeless pets; and as to lovers, she does not dream of them."

Mrs. Braefield, briskly:

"There is no age after six in which girls do not dream of lovers. And here another question arises. When a girl so lovely as Lily is eighteen next birthday, may not a lover dream of her?"

Mrs. Cameron, with that wintry cold tranquillity of manner, which implies that in putting such questions an interrogator is taking a liberty:

"As no lover has appeared, I cannot trouble myself about his dreams."

Said Elsie, inly to herself, "This is the stupidest woman I ever met!" and aloud to Mrs. Cameron:

"Do you not think that your neighbour, Mr. Chillingly, is a very fine young man?"

"I suppose he would be generally considered so. He is very tall."

"A handsome face?"

"Handsome, is it? I dare say."

"What does Lily say?"

"About what?"

"About Mr. Chillingly. Does she not think him handsome?"

"I never asked her."

"My dear Mrs. Cameron, would it not be a very pretty match for Lily? The Chillinglys are among the oldest families in 'Burke's Landed Gentry,' and I believe his father, Sir Peter, has a considerable property."

For the first time in this conversation Mrs. Cameron betrayed emotion. A sudden flush overspread her countenance, and then left it paler than before. After a pause she recovered her accustomed composure, and replied rudely—

"It would be no friend to Lily who could put such notions into her head; and there is no reason to suppose that they have entered into Mr. Chillingly's."

"Would you be sorry if they did? Surely you would like your niece to marry well, and there are few chances of her doing so at Moleswick."

"Pardon me, Mrs. Braefield, but the question of Lily's marriage I have never discussed, even with her guardian. Nor, considering the childlike nature of her tastes and habits, rather than the years she has numbered, can I think the time has yet come for discussing it at all."

Elsie, thus rebuked, changed the subject to some newspaper topic which interested the public mind at the moment, and very soon rose to depart. Mrs. Cameron detained the hand that her visitor held out, and said in low tones, which, though embarrassed, were evidently earnest, "My dear Mrs. Braefield, let me trust to your good sense and the affection with which you have honoured my niece, not to incur the risk of unsettling her mind by a hint of the ambitious projects for her future on which you have spoken to me. It is extremely improbable that a young man of Mr. Chillingly's expectations would entertain any serious thoughts of marrying out of his own sphere of life, and——"

"Stop, Mrs. Cameron. I must interrupt you. Lily's personal attractions and grace of manner would adorn any station; and have I not rightly understood you to say that though her guardian, Mr. Melville, is, as we all know, a man who has risen above the rank of his parents, your niece, Miss Mordaunt, is like yourself, by birth a gentlewoman."

"Yes, by birth a gentlewoman," said Mrs. Cameron, raising her head with a sudden pride. But she added, with as sudden a change to a sort of freezing humility, "what does that matter? A girl without fortune, without connection, brought up in this little cottage, the ward of a professional artist, who was the son of a city clerk, to whom she owes even the home she has found, is not in the same sphere of life as Mr. Chillingly, and his parents could not approve of such an alliance for him. It would be most cruel to her, if you were to change the innocent pleasure she may take in the conversation of a clever and well-informed stranger, into the troubled interest which, since you remind me of her age, a girl even so childlike and beautiful as Lily might conceive in one represented to her as the possible partner of her life. Don't commit that cruelty; don't—don't, I implore you!"

"Trust me," cried the warm-hearted Elsie, with tears rushing to her eyes. "What you say so sensibly, so nobly, never struck me before. I do not know much of the world—knew nothing of it till I married—and being very fond of Lily, and having a strong regard for Mr. Chillingly, I fancied I could not serve both better than—than —but I see now; he is very young, very peculiar; his parents might object, not to Lily herself, but to the circumstances you name. And you would not wish her to enter any family where she was not as cordially welcomed as she deserves to be. I am glad to have had this talk with you. Happily, I have done no mischief as yet. I will do none. I had come to propose an excursion to the remains of the Roman Villa, some miles off, and to invite you and Mr. Chillingly. I will no longer try to bring him and Lily together."

"Thank you. But you still misconstrue me. I do not think that Lily cares half so much for Mr. Chillingly as she does for a new butterfly. I do not fear their coming together, as you call it, in the light in which she now regards him, and in which, from all I observe, he regards her. My only fear is that a hint might lead her to regard him in another way, and that way impossible."

Elsie left the house, extremely bewildered, and with a profound contempt for Mrs. Cameron's knowledge of what may happen to two young persons "brought together."

CHAPTER XVII.

Now, on that very day, and about the same hour in which the conversation just recorded between Elsie and Mrs. Cameron took place, Kenelm, in his solitary noonday wanderings, entered the burial-ground in which Lily had, some short time before, surprised him. And there he found her, standing beside the flower border which she had placed round the grave of the child whom she had tended and nursed in vain.

The day was clouded and sunless; one of those days that so often instil a sentiment of melancholy into the heart of an English summer.

"You come here too often, Miss Mordaunt," said Kenelm very softly, as he approached.

Lily turned her face to him, without any start of surprise, with no brightening change in its pensive expression—an expression rare to the mobile play of her features.

"Not too often. I promised to come as often as I could; and, as I told you before, I have never broken a promise yet."

Kenelm made no answer. Presently the girl turned from the spot, and Kenelm followed her silently till she halted before the old tombstone with its effaced inscription.

"See," she said with a faint smile, "I have put fresh flowers there. Since the day we met in this churchyard, I have thought much of that tomb, so neglected, so forgotten, and—" she paused a moment, and went on abruptly,—"do you not often find that you are much too—what is the word? ah! too egotistical, considering, and pondering, and dreaming greatly too much about yourself?"

"Yes, you are right there; though, till you so accused me, my conscience did not detect it."

"And don't you find that you escape from being so haunted by the thought of yourself, when you think of the dead? they can never have any share in your existence *here*. When you say, 'I shall do this or that to-day;' when you dream, 'I may be this or that to-morrow,' you are thinking and dreaming, all by yourself, for yourself. But you are out of yourself, beyond yourself, when you think and dream of the dead, who can have nothing to do with your to-day or your to-morrow."

As we all know, Kenelm Chillingly made it one of the rules of his life never to be taken by surprise. But when the speech I have written down came from the lips of that tamer of butterflies, he was so startled that all it occurred to him to say, after a long pause, was,

"The dead are the past; and with the past rests all in the present or the future that can take us out of our natural selves. The past decides our present. By the past we divine our future. History, poetry, science, the welfare of states, the advancement of individuals, are all connected with tombstones of which inscriptions are effaced. You are right to honour the mouldered tombstones with fresh flowers. It *is* only in the companionship of the dead that one ceases to be an egotist."

If the imperfectly educated Lily had been above the quick comprehension of the academical Kenelm in her speech, so Kenelm was now above the comprehension of Lily. She too paused before she replied,

"If I knew you better, I think I could understand you better. I wish you knew Lion. I should like to hear you talk with him."

While thus conversing, they had left the burial-ground, and were in the pathway trodden by the common wayfarer.

Lily resumed.

"Yes, I should so like to hear you talk with Lion."

"You mean your guardian, Mr. Melville."

"Yes, you know that."

"And why should you like to hear me talk to him?"

"Because there are some things in which I doubt if he was altogether right, and I would ask you to express my doubts to him; you would, would not you?"

"But why can you not express them yourself to your guardian; are you afraid of him?"

"Afraid, no indeed! But—ah, how many people there are coming this way! There is some tiresome public meeting in the town to-day. Let us take the ferry, the other side of the stream is much pleasanter, we shall have it more to ourselves."

Turning aside to the right while she thus spoke, Lily descended a gradual slope to the margin of the stream, on which they found an old man dozily reclined in his ferry-boat.

As, seated side by side, they were slowly borne over the still waters under a sunless sky, Kenelm would have renewed the subject which his companion had begun, but she shook her head, with a significant glance at the ferryman. Evidently what she had to say was too confidential to admit of a listener, not that the old ferryman seemed likely to take the trouble of listening to any talk that was not addressed to him. Lily soon did address her talk to him—
"So, Brown, the cow has quite recovered."

"Yes, Miss, thanks to you, and God bless you. To think of your beating the old witch like that!"

"'Tis not I who beat the witch, Brown; 'tis the fairy. Fairies, you know, are much more powerful than witches."

"So I find, Miss."

Lily here turned to Kenelm, "Mr. Brown has a very nice milch cow that was suddenly taken very ill, and both he and his wife were convinced that the cow was bewitched."

"Of course it were, that stands to reason. Did not Mother Wright tell my old woman that she would repent of selling milk, and abuse her dreadful; and was not the cow taken with shivers that very night?"

"Gently, Brown. Mother Wright did not say that your wife would repent of selling milk, but of putting water into it."

"And how did she know that, if she was not a witch? We have the best of customers among the gentlefolks, and never an one that complained."

"And," answered Lily to Kenelm, unheeding this last observation, which was made in a sullen manner, "Brown had a horrid notion of enticing Mother Wright into his ferry-boat, and throwing her into the water, in order to break the spell upon the cow. But I consulted the fairies, and gave him a fairy charm to tie round the cow's neck. And the cow is quite well now, you see. So, Brown, there was no necessity to throw Mother Wright into the water, because she said you put some of it into the milk. But," she added, as the boat now touched the opposite bank, "shall I tell you, Brown, what the fairies said to me this morning?"

"Do Miss."

"It was this: If Brown's cow yields milk without any water in it, and if water gets into it when the milk is sold, we, the fairies, will pinch Mr. Brown black and blue; and when Brown has his next fit of rheumatics he must not look to the fairies to charm it away."

Herewith Lily dropped a silver groat into

Brown's hand, and sprang lightly ashore, followed by Kenelm.

"You have quite converted him, not only as to the existence, but as to the beneficial power of fairies," said Kenelm.

"Ah," answered Lily very gravely, "Ah, but would it not be nice if there were fairies still? good fairies, and one could get at them? tell them all that troubles and puzzles us, and win from them charms against the witchcraft we practise on ourselves?"

"I doubt if it would be good for us to rely on such supernatural counsellors. Our own souls are so boundless, that the more we explore them the more we shall find worlds spreading upon worlds into infinities; and among the worlds is Fairyland." He added, inly to himself, "Am I not in Fairyland now?"

"Hush!" whispered Lily. "Don't speak more yet awhile. I am thinking over what you have just said, and trying to understand it."

Thus, walking silently, they gained the little

summer-house which tradition dedicated to the memory of Izaak Walton.

Lily entered it and seated herself, Kenelm took his place beside her. It was a small octagon building which, judging by its architecture, might have been built in the troubled reign of Charles I.; the walls plastered within were thickly covered with names, and dates, and inscriptions, in praise of angling, in tribute to Izaak, or with quotations from his books. On the opposite side they could see the lawn of Grasmere, with its great willows dipping into the water. The stillness of the place, with its associations of the angler's still life, were in harmony with the quiet day, its breezeless air, and cloud-vested sky.

"You were to tell me your doubts in connection with your guardian, doubts if he were right in something which you left unexplained, which you could not yourself explain to him."

Lily started as from thoughts alien to the subject thus reintroduced. "Yes, I cannot mention my doubts to him because they relate to me, and he is so good. I owe him so much that I could not bear to vex him by a word that might seem like reproach or complaint. You remember," here she drew nearer to him; and, with that ingenuous confiding look and movement which had, not unfrequently, enraptured him at the moment, and saddened him on reflection—too ingenuous, too confiding, for the sentiment with which he yearned to inspire her—she turned towards him her frank untimorous eyes, and laid her hand on his arm: "You remember that I said in the burial-ground how much I felt that one is constantly thinking too much of oneself. That must be wrong. In talking to you only about myself I know I am wrong, but I cannot help it, I must do so. Do not think ill of me for it. You see I have not been brought up like other girls. Was my guardian right in that? Perhaps if he had insisted upon not letting me have my own wilful way, if he had made me read the books which Mr. and Mrs. Emlyn wanted to force on me, instead of the poems and fairy tales which he gave me, I should have had so much more to think of that I should have thought less of myself. You said that the dead were the past; one forgets oneself when one thinks of the dead. If I had read more of the past, had more subjects of interest in the dead whose history it tells, surely I should be less shut up, as it were, in my own small, selfish heart! It is only very lately I have thought of this, only very lately that I have felt sorrow and shame in the thought that I am so ignorant of what other girls know, even little Clemmy. And I dare not say this to Lion when I see him next, lest he should blame himself, when he only meant to be kind, and used to say, 'I don't want Fairy to be learned, it is enough for me to think she is happy.' And oh, I was so happy, till—till of late!"

"Because till of late you only knew yourself as a child. But, now that you feel the desire of knowledge, childhood is vanishing. Do not vex yourself. With the mind which nature has bestowed on you, such learning as may fit you to converse with those dreaded 'grown-up folks' will come to you very easily and quickly. You will acquire more in a month now than you would have acquired in a year when you were a child, and task-work was loathed, not courted. Your aunt is evidently well instructed, and if I might venture to talk to her about the choice of books—"

"No, don't do that. Lion would not like it."

"Your guardian would not like you to have the education common to other young ladies?"

"Lion forbade my aunt to teach me much that I rather wished to learn. She wanted to do so, but she has given it up at his wish. She only now teases me with those horrid French verbs, and that I know is a mere make-belief. Of course on Sunday it is different, then I must not read anything but the Bible and sermons. I don't care so much for the sermons as I ought, but I could read the Bible all day, every week-day as well as Sunday; and it is from the Bible that I learn that I ought to think less about myself."

Kenelm involuntarily pressed the little hand that lay so innocently on his arm.

"Do you know the difference between one kind of poetry and another?" asked Lily abruptly.

"I am not sure. I ought to know when one kind is good and another kind is bad. But in that respect I find many people, especially professed critics, who prefer the poetry which I call bad to the poetry I think good."

"The difference between one kind of poetry and another, supposing them both to be good," said Lily positively, and with an air of triumph, "is this—I know, for Lion explained it to me. In one kind of poetry the writer throws himself entirely out of his existence, he puts himself into other existences quite strange to his own. He may be a very good man, and he writes his best poetry about very wicked men; he would not hurt a fly, but he delights in describing murderers. But in the other kind of poetry the writer does not put himself into other existences, he expresses his own joys and sorrows, his own individual heart and mind. If he could not hurt a fly, he certainly could not make himself at home in the cruel heart of a murderer. There, Mr. Chillingly, that is the difference between one kind of poetry and another."

"Very true," said Kenelm, amused by the girl's critical definitions. "The difference between dramatic poetry and lyrical. But may I ask what that definition has to do with the subject into which you so suddenly introduced it?"

"Much—for when Lion was explaining this to my aunt, he said, 'A perfect woman is a poem; but she can never be a poem of the one kind, never can make herself at home in the hearts with which she has no connection, never feel any sympathy with crime and evil; she must be a poem of the other kind, weaving out poetry from her own thoughts and fancies.' And turning to me, he said, smiling, 'That is the poem I wish Lily to be. Too many dry books would only spoil the poem.' And you now see why I am so ignorant, and so unlike other girls, and why Mr. and Mrs. Emlyn look down upon me."

"You wrong at least Mr. Emlyn, for it was he who first said to me, 'Lily Mordaunt is a poem.'"

"Did he? I shall love him for that. How pleased Lion will be!"

"Mr. Melville seems to have an extraordinary influence over your mind," said Kenelm with a jealous pang.

"Of course. I have neither father nor mother, Lion has been both to me. Aunty has often said, 'You cannot be too grateful to your guardian; without him I should have no home to shelter you, no bread to give you.' *He* never said that—he would be very angry with aunty if he knew she had said it. When he does not call me Fairy he calls me Princess. I would not displease him for the world."

"He is very much older than you, old enough to be your father, I hear."

"I dare say. But if he were twice as old I could not love him better."

Kenelm smiled—the jealousy was gone. Certainly not thus could any girl, even Lily, speak of one with whom, however she might love him, she was likely to fall in love.

Lily now rose up, rather slowly and wearily. "It is time to go home, aunty will be wondering what keeps me away—come."

They took their way towards the bridge opposite to Cromwell Lodge.

It was not for some minutes that either broke silence. Lily was the first to do so, and with one of those abrupt changes of topic which were common to the restless play of her secret thoughts.

"You have father and mother still living," Mr. Chillingly.

"Thank Heaven, yes."

"Which do you love the best?"

"That is scarcely a fair question. I love my mother very much; but my father and I understand each other better than——"

"I see—it is so difficult to be understood. No one understands me."

"I think I do."

Lily shook her head, with an energetic movement of dissent.

"At least as well as a man can understand a young lady."

"What sort of young lady is Miss Cecilia Travers?"

"Cecilia Travers! When and how did you ever hear that such a person existed?"

"That big London man whom they called Sir Thomas mentioned her name the day we dined at Braefieldville."

"I remember—as having been at the Court ball."

"He said she was very handsome."

"So she is."

"Is she a poem, too?"

"No; that never struck me."

"Mr. Emlyn, I suppose, would call her perfectly brought up—well educated. He would not raise his eyebrows at her as he does at me, poor me, Cinderella!"

"Ah, Miss Mordaunt, you need not envy her. Again let me say that you could very soon educate yourself to the level of any young ladies who adorn the Court balls."

"Ay; but then I should not be a poem," said Lily, with a shy arch side-glance at his face.

They were now on the bridge, and before

Kenelm could answer Lily resumed quickly, "You need not come any farther, it is out of your way."

"I cannot be so disdainfully dismissed, Miss Mordaunt; I insist on seeing you to, at least your garden gate."

Lily made no objection, and again spoke,

"What sort of country do you live in when at home—is it like this?"

"Not so pretty; the features are larger, more hill and dale and woodland; yet there is one feature in our grounds which reminds me a little of this landscape: a light stream, somewhat wider, indeed, than your brooklet; but here and there the banks are so like those by Cromwell Lodge that I sometimes start and fancy myself at home. I have a strange love for rivulets, and all running waters, and in my foot wanderings I find myself magnetically attracted towards them."

Lily listened with interest, and after a short pause said with a half-suppressed sigh, "Your home is much finer than any place here, even than Braefieldville, is it not? Mrs. Braefield says your father is very rich."

"I doubt if he is richer than Mr. Braefield, and though his house may be larger than Braefieldville, it is not so smartly furnished, and has no such luxurious hot-houses and conservatories. My father's tastes are like mine, very simple. Give him his library, and he would scarcely miss his fortune if he lost it. He has in this one immense advantage over me."

"You would miss fortune?" said Lily quickly.

"Not that; but my father is never tired of books. And shall I own it? there are days when books tire me almost as much as they do you."

They were now at the garden gate. Lily with one hand on the latch held out the other to Kenelm, and her smile lit up the dull sky like a burst of sunshine, as she looked in his face and vanished.

BOOK VII.

CHAPTER I.

KENELM did not return home till dusk, and just as he was sitting down to his solitary meal there was a ring at the bell, and Mrs. Jones ushered in Mr. Thomas Bowles.

Though that gentleman had never written to announce the day of his arrival, he was not the less welcome.

"Only," said Kenelm, "if you preserve the appetite I have lost, I fear you will find meagre fare to-day. Sit down, man."

"Thank you, kindly, but I dined two hours ago in London, and I really can eat nothing more."

Kenelm was too well-bred to press unwelcome hospitalities. In a very few minutes his frugal repast was ended, the cloth removed, the two men were left alone.

"Your room is here, of course, Tom; that was engaged from the day I asked you, but you ought to have given me a line to say when to expect you, so that I could have put our hostess on her mettle as to dinner or supper. You smoke still, of course: light your pipe."

"Thank you, Mr. Chillingly, I seldom smoke now; but if you will excuse a cigar," and Tom produced a very smart cigar-case.

"Do as you would at home. I shall send word to Will Somers that you and I sup there to-morrow. You forgive me for letting out your secret. All straightforward now and henceforth. You come to their hearth as a friend, who will grow dearer to them both every year. Ah, Tom, this love for woman seems to me a very wonderful thing. It may sink a man into such deeps of evil, and lift a man into such heights of good."

"I don't know as to the good," said Tom mournfully, and laying aside his cigar.

"Go on smoking; I should like to keep

you company: can you spare me one of your cigars?"

Tom offered his case. Kenelm extracted a cigar, lighted it, drew a few whiffs, and when he saw that Tom had resumed his own cigar, recommenced conversation.

"You don't know as to the good; but tell me honestly, do you think if you had not loved Jessie Wiles, you would be as good a man as you are now?"

"If I am better than I was, it is not because of my love for the girl."

"What then?"

"The loss of her."

Kenelm started, turned very pale, threw aside the cigar, rose and walked the room to and fro with very quick but very irregular strides.

Tom continued quietly. "Suppose I had won Jessie and married her, I don't think any idea of improving myself would have entered my head. My uncle would have been very much offended at my marrying a day-labourer's daughter, and would not have invited me to Luscombe. I should have remained at Graveleigh, with no ambition of being more than a common farrier, an ignorant, noisy, quarrelsome man; and if I could not have made Jessie as fond of me as I wished, I should not have broken myself of drinking, and I shudder to think what a brute I might have been, when I see in the newspapers an account of some drunken wife-beater. How do we know but what that wife-beater loved his wife dearly before marriage, and she did not care for him? His home was unhappy, and so he took to drink and to wife-beating."

"I was right, then," said Kenelm, halting his strides, "when I told you it would be a miserable fate to be married to a girl whom you loved to distraction, and whose heart you could never warm to you, whose life you could never render happy."

"So right!"

"Let us drop that part of the subject at present," said Kenelm, reseating himself, "and talk about your wish to travel. Though contented that you did not marry Jessie, though you can now, without anguish, greet her as the wife of another, still there are some lingering thoughts of her that make you restless; and you feel that you could more easily wrench yourself from these thoughts in a marked change of scene and adventure, that you might bury them altogether in the soil of a strange land. Is it so?"

"Ay, something of that, sir."

Then Kenelm roused himself to talk of foreign lands, and to map out a plan of travel that might occupy some months. He was pleased to find that Tom had already learned enough of French to make himself understood at least upon commonplace matters, and still more pleased to discover that he had been not only reading the proper guide-books or manuals descriptive of the principal places in Europe worth visiting, but that he had acquired an interest in the places; interest in the fame attached to them by their history in the past, or by the treasures of art they contained.

So they talked far into the night, and when

Tom retired to his room Kenelm let himself out of the house noiselessly, and walked with slow steps towards the old summer-house in which he had sat with Lily. The wind had risen, scattering the clouds that had veiled the preceding day, so that the stars were seen in far chasms of the sky beyond—seen for a while in one place, and when the swift clouds rolled over them there, shining out elsewhere. Amid the varying sounds of the trees, through which swept the night gusts, Kenelm fancied he could distinguish the sigh of the willow on the opposite lawn of Grasmere.

CHAPTER II.

KENELM despatched a note to Will Somers early the next morning, inviting himself and Mr. Bowles to supper that evening. His tact was sufficient to make him aware that in such social meal there would be far less restraint for each and all concerned than in a more formal visit from Tom during the day time; and when Jessie, too, was engaged with customers to the shop.

But he led Tom through the town and showed him the shop itself, with its pretty goods at the plate glass windows, and its general air of prosperous trade; then he carried him off into the lanes and fields of the country, drawing out the mind of his companion, and impressed with great admiration of its marked improvement in culture, and in the trains of thought which culture opens out and enriches.

But throughout all their multiform range of subject, Kenelm could perceive that Tom was still pre-occupied and abstracted; the idea of the coming interview with Jessie weighed upon him.

When they left Cromwell Lodge at nightfall, to repair to the supper at Will's, Kenelm noticed that Bowles had availed himself of the contents of his carpet bag, to make some refined alterations in his dress. The alterations became him.

When they entered the parlour, Will rose from his chair with the evidence of deep emotion on his face, advanced to Tom, took his hand and grasped and dropped it without a word. Jessie saluted both guests alike, with drooping eyelids and an elaborate curtsey. The old mother alone was perfectly self-possessed and up to the occasion.

"I am heartily glad to see you, Mr. Bowles," said she, "and so all three of us are, and ought to be; and if baby was older, there would be four."

"And where on earth have you hidden baby?" cried Kenelm. "Surely he might have been kept up for me to-night, when I was expected; the last time I supped here I took you by surprise, and therefore had no right to complain of baby's want of respect to her parents' friends."

Jessie raised the window-curtain, and pointed to the cradle behind it. Kenelm linked his arm in Tom's, led him to the cradle, and leaving him alone to gaze on the sleeping inmate, seated himself at the table, between old Mrs. Somers and Will. Will's eyes were turned away towards the curtain, Jessie holding its folds aside, and the formidable Tom, who had been the terror of his neighbourhood, bending smiling over the cradle; till at last he laid his large hand on the pillow, gently, timidly, careful not to awake the helpless sleeper, and his lips moved, doubtless with a blessing; then he too came to the table, seating himself, and Jessie carried the cradle upstairs.

Will fixed his keen intelligent eyes on his bygone rival; and noticing the changed expression of the once aggressive countenance, the changed costume in which, without tinge of rustic foppery, there was the token of a certain gravity of station scarcely compatible with a return to old loves and old habits in the village world, the last shadow of jealousy vanished from the clear surface of Will's affectionate nature.

"Mr. Bowles," he exclaimed impulsively, "you have a kind heart and a good heart, and a generous heart. And your coming here to-night on this friendly visit is an honour which—which"—"Which," interrupted Kenelm, compassionating Will's embarrassment, "is on the side of us single men. In this free country a married man who has a male baby may be father to the Lord Chancellor or the Archbishop of Canterbury. But —well, my friends, such a meeting as we have to-night does not come often; and after supper let us celebrate it with a bowl of punch. If we have headaches the next morning none of us will grumble."

Old Mrs. Somers laughed out jovially. "Bless you, sir, I did not think of the punch; I will go and see about it," and, baby's socks still in her hands, she hastened from the room.

What with the supper, what with the punch, and what with Kenelm's art of cheery talk on general subjects, all reserve, all awkwardness, all shyness between the convivialists, rapidly disappeared. Jessie mingled in the talk; perhaps (excepting only Kenelm) she talked more than the others, artlessly, gaily, no vestige of the old coquetry; but, now and then, with a touch of genteel finery, indicative of her rise in life, and of the contact of the fancy shopkeeper with noble customers. It was a pleasant evening—Kenelm had resolved that it should be so. Not a hint of the obligations to Mr. Bowles escaped until Will, following his visitor to the door, whispered to Tom, "You don't want thanks, and I can't express them. But when we say our prayers at night, we have always asked God to bless him who brought us together, and has since made us so prosperous—I mean Mr. Chillingly. To-night there will be another besides him, for whom we shall pray, and for whom baby, when he is older, will pray too."

Therewith Will's voice thickened; and he prudently receded, with no unreasonable fear lest the punch might make him too demonstrative of emotion if he said more.

Tom was very silent on the return to Cromwell Lodge; it did not seem the silence of depressed spirits, but rather of quiet meditation, from which Kenelm did not attempt to rouse him.

It was not till they reached the garden pales of Grasmere that Tom, stopping short, and turning his face to Kenelm, said——

"I am very grateful to you for this evening—very."

"It has revived no painful thoughts, then?"

"No; I feel so much calmer in mind than I ever believed I could have been, after seeing her again."

"Is it possible!" said Kenelm, to himself. "How should I feel if I ever saw in Lily the wife of another man: the mother of his child?" At that question he shuddered, and an involuntary groan escaped from his lips. Just then having, willingly in those precincts, arrested his steps, when Tom paused to address him, something softly touched the arm which he had rested on the garden pale. He looked and saw that it was Blanche. The creature, impelled by its instincts towards night-wanderings, had, somehow or other, escaped from its own bed within the house, and hearing a voice that had grown somewhat familiar to its ear, crept from among the shrubs behind upon the edge of the pale. There it stood, with arched back, purring low as in pleased salutation.

Kenelm bent down and covered with kisses the blue ribbon which Lily's hand had bound round the favourite's neck. Blanche submitted to the caress for a moment, and then catching a slight rustle among the shrubs, made by some awaking bird, sprang into the thick of the quivering leaves and vanished.

Kenelm moved on with a quick impatient stride, and no further words were exchanged between him and his companion till they reached their lodging and parted for the night.

CHAPTER III.

THE next day, towards noon, Kenelm and his visitor, walking together along the brookside, stopped before Izaak Walton's summerhouse, and, at Kenelm's suggestion, entered therein to rest, and more at their ease to continue the conversation they had begun.

"You have just told me," said Kenelm, "that you feel as if a load were taken off your heart, now that you have again met Jessie Somers, and that you find her so changed that she is no longer the woman you loved. As to the change, whatever it be, I own, it seems to me for the better, in person, in manners, in character; of course I should not say this, if I were not convinced of your perfect sincerity when you assured me that you are cured of the old wound. But I feel so deeply interested in the question how a fervent love, once entertained and enthroned in the heart of a man so earnestly affectionate and so warm-blooded as yourself, can be, all of a sudden, at a single interview, expelled or transferred into the calm sentiment of friendship, that I pray you to explain?"

"That is what puzzles me, sir," answered Tom, passing his hand over his forehead. "And I don't know if I can explain it."

"Think over it, and try."

Tom mused for some moments and then began. "You see, sir, that I was a very different man myself when I fell in love with Jessie Wiles, and said 'Come what may that girl shall be my wife. Nobody else shall have her.'"

"Agreed; go on."

"But while I was becoming a different man, when I thought of her—and I was always thinking of her—I still pictured her to myself as the same Jessie Wiles; and though, when I did see her again at Graveleigh, after she had married— the day—"

"You saved her from the insolence of the squire."

"—She was but very recently married. I did not realize her as married. I did not see her husband, and the difference within myself was only then beginning. Well, so all the time I was reading and thinking, and striving to improve my old self at Luscombe, still Jessie Wiles haunted me as the only girl I had ever loved, ever could love; I could not believe it possible that I could ever marry any one else. And lately I have been much pressed to marry some one else; all my family wish it; but the face of Jessie rose up before me, and I said to myself, 'I should be a base man if I married one woman, while I could not get another woman out of my head.' I must see Jessie once more, must learn whether her face is now really the face that haunts me when I sit alone; and I have seen her, and it is not that face; it may be handsomer but it is not a girl's face, it is the face of a wife and a mother. And, last evening, while she was talking with an openheartedness which I had never found in her before, I became strangely conscious of the difference in myself that had been silently at work within the last two years or so. Then, sir, when I was but an ill-conditioned, uneducated, petty village farrier, there was no inequality between me and a peasant girl; or rather, in all things except fortune, the peasant girl was much above me. But last evening I asked myself, on watching her and listening to her talk, 'If Jessie were now free, should I press her to be my wife?' and I answered myself 'No.'"

Kenelm listened with rapt attention, and exclaimed briefly, but passionately, "Why?"

"It seems as if I were giving myself airs to say why. But, sir, lately I have been thrown among persons, women as well as men, of a higher class than I was born in; and in a wife I should want a companion up to their mark, and who would keep me up to mine; and, ah sir, I don't feel as if I could find that companion in Mrs. Somers."

"I understand you now, Tom. But you are spoiling a silly romance of mine. I had fancied the little girl with the flower face would grow up to supply the loss of Jessie; and, I am so ignorant of the human heart, I did think it would take all the years required for the little girl to open into a woman, before the loss of the old love could be supplied. I see now that the poor little child with the flower face has no chance."

"Chance? Why Mr. Chillingly," cried Tom evidently much nettled, "Susy is a dear little thing, but she is scarcely more than a mere charity girl. Sir, when I last saw you in London you touched on that matter as if I were still the village farrier's son who might marry a village labourer's daughter. But," added Tom, softening down his irritated tone of voice, "even if Susy were a lady born, I think a man would make a very great mistake, if he thought he could bring up a little girl to regard him as a father; and then, when she grew up, expect her to accept him as a lover."

"Ah, you think that!" exclaimed Kenelm eagerly, and turning eyes that sparkled with joy towards the lawn of Grasmere. "You think that; it is very sensibly said—well—and you have been pressed to marry, and have hung back till you had seen again Mrs. Somers. Now you will be better disposed to such a step; tell me about it?"

"I said, last evening, that one of the principal capitalists at Luscombe, the leading corn-merchant, had offered to take me into partnership. And, sir, he has an only daughter, she is a very amiable girl, has had a first-rate education, and has such pleasant manners and way of talk, quite a lady. If I married her I should soon be the first man at Luscombe, and Luscombe, as you are no doubt aware, returns two members to Parliament; who knows, but that some day the farrier's son might be—." Tom stopped abruptly—abashed at the aspiring thought which, while speaking, had deepened his hardy colour and flashed from his honest eyes.

"Ah!" said Kenelm, almost mournfully, "Is it so; must each man in his life play many parts? Ambition succeeds to love, the reasoning brain to the passionate heart. True, you are changed; my Tom Bowles is gone."

"Not gone in his undying gratitude to you, sir," said Tom, with great emotion. "Your Tom

Bowles would give up all his dreams of wealth or of rising in life, and go through fire and water to serve the friend who first bid him be a new Tom Bowles! Don't despise me as your own work: you said to me that terrible day, when madness was on my brow and crime within my heart, 'I will be to you the truest friend man ever found in man.' So you have been. You commanded me to read, you commanded me to think, you taught me that body should be the servant of mind."

"Hush, hush, times are altered; it is you who can teach me now. Teach me, teach me; how does ambition replace love? How does the desire to rise in life become the all-mastering passion, and, should it prosper, the all-atoning consolation of our life? We can never be as happy, though we rose to the throne of the Cæsars, as we dream that we could have been, had Heaven but permitted us to dwell in the obscurest village, side by side with the woman we love."

Tom was exceedingly startled by such a burst of irrepressible passion from the man who had told him, that, though friends were found only once in a life, sweethearts were as plentiful as blackberries.

Again he swept his hand over his forehead, and replied hesitatingly. "I can't pretend to say what may be the case with others. But to judge by my own case it seems to be this: a young man who, out of his own business, has nothing to interest or excite him, finds content, interest, and excitement when he falls in love; and then, whether for good or ill, he thinks there is nothing like love in the world, he don't care a fig for ambition then. Over and over again did my poor uncle ask me to come to him at Luscombe, and represent all the worldly advantage it would be to me; but I could not leave the village in which Jessie lived, and besides, I felt myself unfit to be anything higher than I was. But when I had been some time at Luscombe, and gradually got accustomed to another sort of people, and another sort of talk, then I began to feel interest in the same objects that interested those about me; and when, partly by mixing with better educated men, and partly by the pains I took to educate myself, I felt that I might now more easily rise above my uncle's rank of life than two years ago I could have risen above a farrier's forge, then the ambition to rise did stir in me and grew stronger every day. Sir, I don't think you can wake up a man's intellect but what you wake with it emulation. And after all emulation is ambition."

"Then I suppose I have no emulation in me, for certainly I have no ambition."

"That I can't believe, sir, other thoughts may cover it over and keep it down for a time. But sooner or later, it will force its way to the top, as it has done with me. To get on in life, to be respected by those who know you, more and more as you grow older, I call that a manly desire. I am sure it comes as naturally to an Englishman as—as——"

"As the wish to knock down some other Englishman who stands in his way, does. I perceive now that you were always a very ambitious man, Tom; the ambition has only taken another direction. Cæsar might have been

'But the first wrestler on the green.'

"And now, I suppose, you abandon the idea of travel; you will return to Luscombe, cured of all regret for the loss of Jessie; you will marry the young lady you mention, and rise through progressive steps of alderman and mayor into the rank of member for Luscombe."

"All that may come in good time," answered Tom, not resenting the tone of irony in which he was addressed, "but I still intend to travel; a year so spent must render me all the more fit for any station I aim at. I shall go back to Luscombe to arrange my affairs, come to terms with Mr. Leland the corn-merchant against my return, and——"

"The young lady is to wait till then."

"Emily."

"Oh, that is the name? Emily! a much more elegant name than Jessie."

"Emily," continued Tom, with an unruffled placidity, which, considering the aggravating bitterness for which Kenelm had exchanged his wonted dulcitudes of indifferentism, was absolutely saintlike, "Emily knows that if she were my wife I should be proud of her, and will esteem me the more if she feels how resolved I am that she shall never be ashamed of me."

"Pardon me, Tom," said Kenelm, softened and laying his hand on his friend's shoulder with brother-like tenderness. "Nature has made you a thorough gentleman; and you could not think and speak more nobly if you had come into the world as the head of all the Howards."

CHAPTER IV.

TOM went away the next morning. He declined to see Jessie again, saying curtly, "I don't wish the impression made on me the other evening to incur a chance of being weakened."

Kenelm was in no mood to regret his friend's departure. Despite all the improvement in Tom's manners and culture, which raised him so much nearer to equality with the polite and instructed heir of the Chillinglys, Kenelm would have felt more in sympathy, and *rapport*, with the old disconsolate fellow-wanderer who had reclined with him on the grass, listening to the Minstrel's talk or verse, than he did with the practical, rising citizen of Luscombe. To the young lover of Lily Mordaunt there was a discord, a jar, in the knowledge that the human heart admits of such well-reasoned, well-justified transfers of allegiance; a

Jessie to-day, or an Emily to-morrow— "*La reine est morte; vive la reine.*"

An hour or two after Tom had gone, Kenelm found himself almost mechanically led towards Braefieldville. He had instinctively divined Elsie's secret wish with regard to himself and Lily, however skilfully she thought she had concealed it.

At Braefieldville he should hear talk of Lily, and in the scenes where Lily had been first beheld.

He found Mrs. Braefield alone in the drawing-room, seated by a table covered with flowers, which she was assorting and intermixing for the vases to which they were destined.

It struck him that her manner was more reserved than usual and somewhat embarrassed; and when, after a few preliminary matters of small talk, he rushed boldly *in medias res*, and asked if she had seen Mrs. Cameron lately? She replied briefly, "Yes, I called there the other day," and immediately changed the conversation to the troubled state of the Continent.

Kenelm was resolved not to be so put off, and presently returned to the charge.

"The other day you proposed an excursion to the site of the Roman villa, and said you would ask Mrs. Cameron to be of the party. Perhaps you have forgotten it?"

"No; but Mrs. Cameron declines. We can ask the Emlyns instead. He will be an excellent *cicerone.*"

"Excellent! Why did Mrs. Cameron decline?"

Elsie hesitated, and then lifted her clear brown eyes to his face, with a sudden determination to bring matters to a crisis.

"I cannot say why Mrs. Cameron declined, but in declining she acted very wisely and very honourably. Listen to me, Mr. Chillingly. You know how highly I esteem, and how cordially I like you, and judging by what I felt for some weeks, perhaps longer, after we parted at Tor-Hadham—" Here again she hesitated, and with a half laugh and a slight blush, again went resolutely on. "If I were Lily's aunt or elder sister, I should do as Mrs. Cameron does; decline to let Lily see much more of a young gentleman too much above her in wealth and station for—"

"Stop," cried Kenelm haughtily, "I cannot allow that any man's wealth or station would warrant his presumption in thinking himself above Miss Mordaunt."

"Above her in natural grace and refinement, certainly not. But in the world there are other considerations which, perhaps, Sir Peter and Lady Chillingly might take into account."

"You did not think of that before you last saw Mrs. Cameron."

"Honestly speaking, I did not. Assured that Miss Mordaunt was a gentlewoman by birth, I did not sufficiently reflect upon other disparities."

"You know, then, that she is by birth a gentlewoman?"

"I only know it as all here do, by the assurance of Mrs. Cameron, whom no one could suppose not to be a lady. But there are different degrees of lady and of gentleman, which are little heeded in the ordinary intercourse of

society, but become very perceptible in questions
of matrimonial alliance; and Mrs. Cameron herself says very plainly that she does not consider
her niece to belong to that station in life from
which Sir Peter and Lady Chillingly would
naturally wish their son should select his bride.
Then (holding out her hand) pardon me if I
have wounded or offended you. I speak as a
true friend to you and to Lily both. Earnestly
I advise you, if Miss Mordaunt be the cause of
your lingering here, earnestly I advise you to
leave while yet in time for her peace of mind
and your own."

"Her peace of mind," said Kenelm, in low
faltering tones, scarcely hearing the rest of Mrs.
Braefield's speech. "Her peace of mind. Do
you sincerely think that she cares for me—could
care for me—if I staid?"

"I wish I could answer you decidedly. I am
not in the secrets of her heart. I can but conjecture that it might be dangerous for the peace
of any young girl to see too much of a man like
yourself, to divine that he loved her, and not to

be aware that he could not, with the approval of his family, ask her to become his wife."

Kenelm bent his face down, and covered it with his right hand. He did not speak for some moments. Then he rose, the fresh cheek very pale, and said—

"You are right. Miss Mordaunt's peace of mind must be the first consideration. Excuse me if I quit you thus abruptly. You have given me much to think of, and I can only think of it adequately when alone."

CHAPTER V.

FROM Kenelm Chillingly to Sir Peter Chillingly.

"MY FATHER, MY DEAR FATHER,—This is no reply to your letters. I know not if itself can be called a letter. I cannot yet decide whether it be meant to reach your hands. Tired with talking to myself, I sit down to talk to you. Often have I reproached myself for not seizing every fitting occasion to let you distinctly know how warmly I love, how deeply I reverence you; you, O friend, O father. But we Chillinglys are not a demonstrative race. I don't remember that you, by words, ever expressed to me the truth that you love your son infinitely more than he deserves. Yet, do I not know that you would send all your beloved old books to the hammer, rather than I should pine in vain for some untried, if sinless, delight on which I had set my heart? And do you not know, equally well, that I would part with all my heritage, and turn day-labourer, rather than you should miss the beloved old books?

"That mutual knowledge is taken for granted in all that my heart yearns to pour forth to your own. But, if I divine aright, a day is coming when, as between you and me, there must be a sacrifice on the part of one to the other. If so, I implore that the sacrifice may come from you. How is this? How am I so ungenerous, so egotistical, so selfish, so ungratefully unmindful of all I already owe to you, and may never repay? I can only answer, 'It is fate, it is nature, it is love'—

* * * *

"Here I must break off.. It is midnight, the moon halts opposite to the window at which I sit, and on the stream that runs below there is a long narrow track on which every wave trembles in her light; on either side of the moonlit track all the other waves, running equally to their grave in the invisible deep, seem motionless and dark. I can write no more."

* * * *

Dated two days later.

"THEY say she is beneath us in wealth and station. Are we, my father—we, two well-born gentlemen—coveters of gold or lackeys of the great? When I was at College, if there were any there more heartily despised than another, it was the parasite and the tuft-hunter; the man who chose his friends according as their money or their rank might be of use to him. If so mean where the choice is so little important to the happiness and career of a man who has something of manhood in him, how much more mean to be the parasite and tuft-hunter in deciding what woman to love, what woman to select as the sweetener and ennobler of one's everyday life! Could she be to my life that sweetener, that ennobler? I firmly believe it. Already life itself has gained a charm that I never even guessed in it before; already I begin, though as yet but faintly and vaguely, to recognise that

interest in the objects and aspirations of my
fellow-men, which is strongest in those whom
posterity ranks among its ennoblers. In this
quiet village it is true that I might find examples
enough to prove that man is not meant to meditate
upon life, but to take active part in it, and in
that action to find his uses. But I doubt if I
should have profited by such examples; if I
should not have looked on this small stage of
the world as I have looked on the large one,
with the indifferent eyes of a spectator on a trite
familiar play carried on by ordinary actors, had
not my whole being suddenly leapt out of
philosophy into passion, and, at once made
warmly human, sympathized with humanity
wherever it burned and glowed. Ah, is there to
be any doubt of what station, as mortal bride, is
due to her—her, my princess, my Fairy? If so,
how contented you shall be, my father, with the
worldly career of your son! how perseveringly he
will strive (and when did perseverance fail?) to
supply all his deficiencies of intellect, genius,
knowledge, by the energy concentrated on a single

object which—more than intellect, genius, knowledge, unless they attain to equal energy equally concentrated—commands what the world calls honours.

"Yes, with her, with her as the bearer of my name, with her to whom I, whatever I might do of good or of great, could say, 'It is thy work,' I promise that you shall bless the day when you took to your arms a daughter.

* * * *

"'Thou art in contact with the beloved in all that thou feelest elevated above thêe.' So is it written by one of those weird Germans who search in our bosoms for the seeds of buried truths, and conjure them into flowers before we ourselves were even aware of the seeds.

"Every thought that associates itself with my beloved seems to me born with wings.

* * * *

I have just seen her, just parted from her. Since I had been told—kindly, wisely told—that I had no right to hazard her peace of mind unless I were privileged to woo and to win her, I promised myself that I would shun her presence until I had bared my heart to you, as I am doing now, and received that privilege from yourself; for even had I never made the promise that binds my honour, your consent and blessing must hallow my choice. I do not feel as if I could dare to ask one so innocent and fair to wed an ungrateful, disobedient son. But this evening I met her, unexpectedly, at the vicar's, an excellent man, from whom I have learned much; whose precepts, whose example, whose delight in his home, and his life at once active and serene, are in harmony with my own dreams when I dream of her.

"I will tell you the name of the beloved—hold, it is as yet a profound secret between you and me. But oh for the day when I may hear you call her by that name, and print on her forehead the only kiss by man of which I should not be jealous.

"It is Sunday, and after the evening service it is my friend's custom to gather his children round him, and, without any formal sermon or discourse, engage their interest in subjects harmonious to associations with the sanctity of the day; often not directly bearing upon religion; more often, indeed, playfully starting from some little incident or some slight story book which had amused the children in the course of the past week, and then gradually winding into reference to some sweet moral precept or illustration from some divine example. It is a maxim with him that, while much that children must learn they can only learn well through conscious labour, and as positive task-work, yet Religion should be connected in their minds, not with labour and task-work, but should become insensibly infused into their habits of thought, blending itself with memories and images of peace and love; with the indulgent tenderness of the earliest teachers, the sinless mirthfulness of the earliest home; with consolation in after sorrows, support through after trials, and never parting company with its twin sister, Hope.

"I entered the vicar's room this evening just as the group had collected round him. By the

side of his wife sat a lady in whom I feel a keen
interest. Her face wears that kind of calm which
speaks of the lassitude bequeathed by sorrow.
She is the aunt of my beloved one. Lily had
nestled herself on a low ottoman, at the good
pastor's feet, with one of his little girls, round
whose shoulder she had wound her arm. She is
much more fond of the companionship of children than that of girls of her own age. The
vicar's wife, a very clever woman, once, in my
hearing, took her to task for this preference, asking her why she persisted in grouping herself
with mere infants who could teach her nothing?
Ah! could you have seen the innocent, angel-like
expression of her face when she answered simply,
'I suppose because with them I feel safer, I mean
nearer to God.'

"Mr. Emlyn—that is the name of the vicar
—deduced his homily this evening from a pretty
fairy tale which Lily had been telling to his
children the day before, and which he drew her
on to repeat.

"Take, in brief, the substance of the story:—

"'Once on a time, a king and queen made themselves very unhappy because they had no heir to their throne; and they prayed for one; and lo, on some bright summer morning, the Queen, waking from sleep, saw a cradle beside her bed, and in the cradle a beautiful sleeping babe. Great day throughout the kingdom! But as the infant grew up, it became very wayward and fretful; it lost its beauty, it would not learn its lessons, it was as naughty as a child could be. The parents were very sorrowful; the heir, so longed for, promised to be a great plague to themselves and their subjects. At last one day, to add to their trouble, two little bumps appeared on the Prince's shoulders. All the doctors were consulted as to the cause and the cure of this deformity. Of course they tried the effect of back-bands and steel machines, which gave the poor little Prince great pain, and made him more unamiable than ever. The bumps, nevertheless, grew larger, and as they increased, so the Prince sickened and pined away. At last a skilful surgeon proposed, as the only chance of saving the

Prince's life, that the bumps should be cut out, and the next morning was fixed for that operation. But at night the Queen saw, or dreamed she saw, a beautiful shape standing by her bedside. And it said to her reproachfully, 'Ungrateful woman! How wouldst thou repay me for the precious boon that my favour bestowed on thee? In me behold the Queen of the Fairies. For the heir to thy kingdom, I consigned to thy charge an infant from Fairyland, to become a blessing to thee and to thy people; and thou wouldst inflict upon it a death of torture by the surgeon's knife.' And the Queen answered: 'Precious indeed thou mayest call the boon! A miserable, sickly, feverish changeling.'

"'Art thou so dull,' said the beautiful visitant, 'as not to comprehend that the earliest instincts of the fairy child would be those of discontent, at the exile from its native home? and in that discontent it would have pined itself to death, or grown up, soured and malignant, a fairy still in its power but a fairy of wrath and evil, had not the strength of its inborn nature sufficed to develop the growth of its wings. That which thy blindness condemns as the deformity of the human-born, is to the fairy-born the crowning perfection of its beauty. Woe to thee, if thou suffer not the wings of the fairy child to grow.'

"'And the next morning the Queen sent away the surgeon when he came with his horrible knife, and removed the back-board and the steel machines from the Prince's shoulders, though all the doctors predicted that the child would die. And from that moment the royal heir began to recover bloom and health. And when at last, out of those deforming bumps, budded delicately forth the plumage of snow-white wings, the wayward peevishness of the Prince gave place to sweet temper. Instead of scratching his teachers, he became the quickest and most docile of pupils, grew up to be the joy of his parents and the pride of their people; and the people said, 'In him we shall have hereafter such a king as we have never yet known.'

"Here ended Lily's tale. I cannot convey to you a notion of the pretty, playful manner in which it was told. Then she said, with a grave shake of the head, 'But you do not seem to know what happened afterwards. Do you suppose that the Prince never made use of his wings? Listen to me. It was discovered by the courtiers who attended on his Royal Highness that on certain nights, every week, he disappeared. In fact, on these nights, obedient to the instinct of the wings, he flew from palace halls into Fairyland; coming back thence all the more lovingly disposed towards the human home from which he had escaped for awhile.'

"'Oh my children,' interposed the preacher earnestly, 'the wings would be given to us in vain if we did not obey the instinct which allures us to soar; vain, no less, would be the soaring, were it not towards the home whence we came, bearing back from its native airs a stronger health, and a serener joy; more reconciled to the duties of earth by every new flight into heaven.'

"As he thus completed the moral of Lily's fairy tale, the girl rose from her low seat, took his hand, kissed it reverently, and walked away towards the window. I could see that she was affected even to tears, which she sought to conceal. Later in the evening, when we were dispersed on the lawn, for a few minutes before the party broke up, Lily came to my side timidly and said, in a low whisper:

"'Are you angry with me? what have I done to displease you?'

"'Angry with you; displeased? How can you think of me so unjustly?'

"'It is so many days since you have called, since I have seen you,' she said, so artlessly, looking up at me with eyes in which tears still seemed to tremble.

"Before I could trust myself to reply, her aunt approached, and noticing me with a cold and distant 'Good night,' led away her niece.

"I had calculated on walking back to their home with them, as I generally have done when we met at another house. But the aunt had probably conjectured I might be at the vicarage that evening, and in order to frustrate my intention, had engaged a carriage for their return. No doubt she has been warned against permitting further intimacy with her niece.

"My father, I must come to you at once, discharge my promise, and receive from your own lips your consent to my choice; for you will consent, will you not? But I wish you to be prepared beforehand, and I shall therefore put up these disjointed fragments of my commune with my own heart and with yours, and post them to-morrow. Expect me to follow them, after leaving you a day free to consider them alone—alone, my dear father; they are meant for no eye but yours.   "K. C."

CHAPTER VI.

The next day Kenelm walked into the town, posted his voluminous letter to Sir Peter, and then looked in at the shop of Will Somers, meaning to make some purchases of basket-work or trifling fancy goods in Jessie's pretty store of such articles, that might please the taste of his mother.

On entering the shop his heart beat quicker. He saw two young forms bending over the counter, examining the contents of a glass case. One of these customers was Clemmy; in the other there was no mistaking the slight graceful shape of Lily Mordaunt. Clemmy was exclaiming, "Oh it is so pretty, Mrs. Somers; but," turning her eyes from the counter to a silk purse in her hand, she added sorrowfully, "I can't buy it. I have not got enough, not by a great deal."

"And what is it, Miss Clemmy?" asked Kenelm.

The two girls turned round at his voice, and Clemmy's face brightened.

"Look here," she said, "is it not too lovely?"

The object thus admired and coveted was a little gold-locket, enriched by a cross composed of small pearls.

"I assure you, miss," said Jessie, who had acquired all the coaxing arts of her trade, "it is really a great bargain. Miss Mary Burrows, who was here just before you came, bought one not nearly so pretty, and gave ten shillings more for it."

Miss Mary Burrows was the same age as Miss Clementina Emlyn, and there was a rivalry as to smartness between those youthful beauties. "Miss Burrows!" sighed Clemmy very scornfully.

But Kenelm's attention was distracted from Clemmy's locket to a little ring which Lily had been persuaded by Mrs. Somers to try on, and which she now drew off and returned with a shake of the head. Mrs. Somers, who saw that she had small chance of selling the locket to Clemmy, was now addressing herself to the elder girl more likely to have sufficient pocket-money, and whom, at all events, it was quite safe to trust.

"The ring fits you so nicely, Miss Mordaunt, and every young lady of your age wears at least one ring; allow me to put it up?" She added in a lower voice, "Though we only sell the articles in this case on commission, it is all the same to us whether we are paid now or at Christmas."

"'Tis no use tempting me, Mrs. Somers," said Lily, laughing, and then with a grave air, "I promised Lion, I mean my guardian, never to run into debt, and I never will."

Lily turned resolutely from the perilous counter, taking up a paper that contained a new ribbon she had bought for Blanche, and Clemmy reluctantly followed her out of the shop.

Kenelm lingered behind and selected very hastily a few trifles, to be sent to him that evening with some specimens of basket-work left to Will's tasteful discretion; then purchased the locket on which Clemmy had set her heart; but all the while his thoughts were fixed on the ring which Lily had tried on. It was no sin against etiquette to give the locket to a child like Clemmy, but would it not be a cruel impertinence to offer a gift to Lily?

Jessie spoke:

"Miss Mordaunt took a great fancy to this ring, Mr. Chillingly. I am sure her aunt would like her to have it. I have a great mind to put it by on the chance of Mrs. Cameron's calling here. It would be a pity if it were bought by some one else."

"I think," said Kenelm, "that I will take the liberty of showing it to Mrs. Cameron. No doubt she will buy it for her niece. Add the price of it to my bill." He seized the ring and carried it off; a very poor little simple ring, with a single stone, shaped as a heart, not half the price of the locket.

Kenelm rejoined the young ladies just where the path split into two, the one leading direct to Grasmere, the other through the churchyard to the Vicarage. He presented the locket to Clemmy with brief kindly words which easily removed any scruple she might have had in accepting it; and, delighted with her acquisition, she bounded off to the Vicarage, impatient to show the prize to her mamma and sisters, and more especially to Miss Mary Burrows, who was coming to lunch with them.

Kenelm walked on slowly by Lily's side.

"You have a good heart, Mr. Chillingly," said she, somewhat abruptly. "How it must please you to give such pleasure! Dear little Clemmy!"

This artless praise, and the perfect absence of envy or thought of self evinced by her joy that her friend's wish was gratified, though her own was not, enchanted Kenelm.

"If it pleases to give pleasure," said he, "it is your turn to be pleased now, you can confer such pleasure upon me."

"How?" she asked, falteringly and with quick change of colour.

"By conceding to me the same right your little friend has allowed."

And he drew forth the ring.

Lily reared her head with a first impulse of haughtiness. But when her eyes met his the head drooped down again, and a slight shiver ran through her frame.

"Miss Mordaunt," resumed Kenelm, mastering his passionate longing to fall at her feet and say, "But, oh! in this ring it is my love that I offer—it is my troth that I pledge!" "Miss Mordaunt, spare me the misery of thinking that I have offended you; least of all would I do so on this day, for it may be some little while before I see you again. I am going home for a few days upon a matter which may affect the happiness of my life, and on which I should be a bad son and an unworthy gentleman if I did not consult him who, in all that concerns my affections has trained me to turn to him, the father; in all that concerns my honour to him, the gentleman."

A speech more unlike that which any delineator of manners and morals in the present day would put into the mouth of a lover, no critic in the 'Londoner' could ridicule. But, somehow or other, this poor little tamer of butterflies and teller of fairy tales comprehended on the instant all that this most eccentric of human beings thus frigidly left untold. Into her innermost heart it sank more deeply than would the most ardent declaration put into the lips of the boobies or the scamps in whom delineators of manners in the present day too often debase the magnificent chivalry embodied in the name of 'Lover.'

Where these two had, while speaking, halted on the path along the brookside, there was a bench, on which it so happened that they had seated themselves weeks before. A few moments later on that bench they were seated again.

And the trumpery little ring with its turquoise heart was on Lily's finger, and there they continued to sit for nearly half an hour; not talking much, but wondrously happy; not a single vow of troth interchanged. No, not even a word that could be construed into "I love." And yet when they rose from the bench, and went silently along the brookside, each knew that the other was beloved.

When they reached the gate that admitted into the garden of Grasmere, Kenelm made a slight start. Mrs. Cameron was leaning over the gate. Whatever alarm at the appearance Kenelm might have felt was certainly not shared by Lily; she advanced lightly before him, kissed her aunt on the cheek, and passed on across the lawn with a bound in her step and the carol of a song upon her lips.

Kenelm remained by the gate, face to face with Mrs. Cameron. She opened the gate, put her arm in his, and led him back along the brookside.

"I am sure, Mr. Chillingly," she said, "that you will not impute to my words any meaning more grave than that which I wish them to convey, when I remind you that there is no place too obscure to escape from the ill-nature of gossip, and you must own that my niece incurs the chance of its notice if she be seen walking alone in these by-paths with a man of your age and position, and whose sojourn in the neighbourhood, without any ostensible object or motive, has already begun to excite conjecture. I do not for a moment assume that you regard my niece in any other light than that of an artless child whose originality of tastes or fancy may serve to amuse you; and still less do I suppose that she is in danger of misrepresenting any attentions on your part. But for her sake I am bound to consider what others may say. Excuse me then if I add that I think you are also bound in honour and in good feeling to do the same. Mr. Chillingly, it would give me a great sense of relief if it suited your plans to move from the neighbourhood."

"My dear Mrs. Cameron," answered Kenelm, who had listened to this speech with imperturbable calm of visage; "I thank you much for your candour, and I am glad to have this opportunity of informing you that I am about to move from this neighbourhood, with the hope of returning to it in a very few days and rectifying your mistake as to the point of view in which I regard your niece. In a word," here the expression of his countenance and the tone of his voice underwent a sudden change, "it is the dearest wish of my heart to be empowered by my parents to assure you of the warmth with which they will welcome your niece as their daughter, should she deign to listen to my suit and entrust me with the charge of her happiness."

Mrs. Cameron stopped short, gazing into his face with a look of inexpressible dismay.

"No! Mr. Chillingly," she exclaimed, "this must not be—cannot be. Put out of your mind an idea so wild. A young man's senseless romance. Your parents cannot consent to your union with my niece; I tell you beforehand they cannot."

"But why?" said Kenelm, with a slight smile, and not much impressed by the vehemence of Mrs. Cameron's adjuration.

"Why?" she repeated passionately; and then recovering something of her habitual weariness of quiet. "The why is easily explained. Mr. Kenelm Chillingly is the heir of a very ancient house and, I am told, of considerable estates. Lily Mordaunt is a nobody, an orphan, without fortune, without connexion, the ward of a humbly born artist, to whom she owes the roof that shelters her; she is without the ordinary education of a gentlewoman; she has seen nothing of the world in which you move. Your parents have not the right to allow a son so young as yourself to throw himself out of his proper sphere by a rash and imprudent alliance. And, never would I consent, never would Walter Melville consent, to her entering into any family reluctant to receive her. There—that is enough. Dismiss the notion so lightly entertained. And farewell."

"Madam," answered Kenelm very earnestly, "believe me, that had I not entertained the hope approaching to conviction that the reasons you urge against my presumption will not have the weight with my parents which you ascribe to them, I should not have spoken to you thus frankly. Young though I be, still I might fairly claim the right to choose for myself in marriage.

But I gave to my father a very binding promise that I would not formally propose to any one till I had acquainted him with my desire to do so, and obtained his approval of my choice; and he is the last man in the world who would withhold that approval where my heart is set on it as it is now. I want no fortune with a wife, and should I ever care to advance my position in the world no connexion could help me like the approving smile of the woman I love. There is but one qualification which my parents would deem they had the right to exact from my choice of one who is to bear our name. I mean that she should have the appearance, the manners, the principles — and my mother at least might add — the birth of a gentlewoman. Well, as to appearance and manners, I have seen much of fine society from my boyhood, and found no one among the highest born who can excel the exquisite refinement of every look, and the inborn delicacy of every thought, in her of whom, if mine, I shall be as proud as I shall be fond. As to defects in the frippery and tinsel of a boarding-school education, they are very soon remedied. Remains only the last consideration —birth. Mrs. Braefield informs me that you have assured her that, though circumstances into which as yet I have no right to inquire, have made her the ward of a man of humble origin, Miss Mordaunt is of gentle birth. Do you deny that?"

"No," said Mrs. Cameron, hesitating, but with a flash of pride in her eyes as she went on. "No. I cannot deny that my niece is descended from those who, in point of birth, were not unequal to your own ancestors. But what of that?" she added, with a bitter despondency of tone. "Equality of birth ceases when one falls into poverty, obscurity, neglect, nothingness!"

"Really this is a morbid habit on your part. But since we have thus spoken so confidentially, will you not empower me to answer the question which will probably be put to me, and the answer to which will, I doubt not, remove every obstacle in the way of my happiness. Whatever the reasons which might very sufficiently induce you to preserve, whilst living so quietly in this place, a discreet silence as to the parentage of Miss Mordaunt and your own—and I am well aware that those whom altered circumstances of fortune have compelled to altered modes of life, may disdain to parade to strangers the pretensions to a higher station than that to which they reconcile their habits—whatever, I say, such reasons for silence to strangers, should they preclude you from confiding to me, an aspirant to your niece's hand, a secret which, after all, cannot be concealed from her future husband?"

"From her future husband? of course not," answered Mrs. Cameron. "But I decline to be questioned by one whom I may never see again, and of whom I know so little. I decline, indeed, to assist in removing any obstacle to an union with my niece, which I hold to be in every way unsuited to either party. I have no cause even to believe that my niece would accept you if you were free to propose to her. You have not, I presume, spoken to her as an aspirant to her hand. You have not addressed to her any declaration of your attachment, or sought to extract from her inexperience any words that warrant you in thinking that her heart will break if she never sees you again."

"I do not merit such cruel and taunting questions," said Kenelm indignantly. "But I will say no more now. When we again meet let me hope you will treat me less unkindly. Adieu!"

"Stay, sir. A word or two more. You persist in asking your father and Lady Chillingly to consent to your proposal to Miss Mordaunt?"

"Certainly I do."

"And you will promise me, on your word as a gentleman, to state fairly all the causes which might fairly operate against their consent; the poverty, the humble rearing, the imperfect education of my niece; so that they might not hereafter say you had entrapped their consent, and avenge themselves for your deceit by contempt for her?"

"Ah, madam, madam, you really try my patience too far. But take my promise, if you can hold that of value from one whom you can suspect of deliberate deceit."

"I beg your pardon, Mr. Chillingly. Bear with my rudeness. I have been so taken by surprise I scarcely know what I am saying. But let us understand each other completely before we part. If your parents withhold their consent you will communicate it to me; me only, not to Lily. I repeat I know nothing of the state of her affections. But it might embitter any girl's life to be led on to love one whom she could not marry."

"It shall be as you say. But if they do consent?"

"Then you will speak to me before you seek an interview with Lily, for then comes another question: Will her guardian consent?—and—and—"

"And what?"

"No matter. I rely on your honour in this request, as in all else. Good-day."

She turned back with hurried footsteps, muttering to herself, "But they will not consent. Heaven grant that they will not consent, or if they do, what—what is to be said or done? Oh, that Walter Melville were here, or that I knew where to write to him!"

On his way back to Cromwell Lodge Kenelm was overtaken by the vicar.

"I was coming to you, my dear Mr. Chillingly, first to thank you for the very pretty present with which you have gladdened the heart of my little Clemmy, and next to ask you to come with me quietly to-day to meet Mr.——, the celebrated antiquarian, who came to Moleswick this morning at my request, to examine that old gothic tomb in our churchyard. Only think,—though he cannot read the inscription any better than we can, he knows all about its history. It seems that a young knight renowned for feats of valour in the reign of Henry IV. married a daughter of one of those great Earls of Montfichet who were then the most powerful family in these parts. He was slain in defending the church from an assault by some disorderly rioters of the Lollard faction; he fell on the very spot where the tomb is now placed. That accounts for its situation in the churchyard, not within the fabric. Mr. —— discovered this fact in an old memoir of the ancient and once famous family to which the young knight Albert belonged, and which came, alas! to so shameful an end, the Fletwodes, Barons of Fletwode and Malpas. What a triumph over pretty Lily Mordaunt, who always chose to imagine that the tomb must be that of some heroine of her own romantic invention! Do come to dinner; Mr. —— is a most agreeable man, and full of interesting anecdote."

"I am so sorry I cannot. I am obliged to return home at once for a few days. That old family of Fletwode! I think I see before me, while we speak, the grey tower in which they once held sway; and the last of the race following Mammon along the Progress of the Age—a convicted felon! What a terrible satire on the pride of birth!"

Kenelm left Cromwell Lodge that evening, but he still kept on his apartments there, saying he might be back unexpectedly any day in the course of the next week.

He remained two days in London, wishing all that he had communicated to Sir Peter in writing to sink into his father's heart before a personal appeal to it.

The more he revolved the ungracious manner in which Mrs. Cameron had received his confidence, the less importance he attached to it. An exaggerated sense of disparities of fortune in a person who appeared to him to have the pride so common to those who have known better days, coupled with a nervous apprehension lest his family should ascribe to her any attempt to ensnare a very young man of considerable worldly pretensions into a marriage with a penniless niece, seemed to account for much that had at first perplexed and angered him. And if, as he conjectured, Mrs. Cameron had once held a much higher position in the world than she did now— a conjecture warranted by a certain peculiar conventional undeniable elegance which characterized her habitual manner—and was now, as she implied, actually a dependant on the bounty of a painter who had only just acquired some professional distinction, she might well shrink from the mortification of becoming an object of compassion to her richer neighbours; nor, when he came to think of it, had he any more right than those neighbours to any confidence as to her own or Lily's parentage, so long as he was not formally entitled to claim admission into her privity.

London seemed to him intolerably dull and wearisome. He called nowhere except at Lady Glenalvon's: he was glad to hear from the servants that she was still at Exmundham. He relied much on the influence of the queen of the Fashion with his mother, whom he knew would be more difficult to persuade than Sir Peter, nor did he doubt that he should win to his side that sympathizing and warm-hearted queen.

CHAPTER VII.

It is somewhere about three weeks since the party invited by Sir Peter and Lady Chillingly assembled at Exmundham, and they are still there, though people invited to a country house have seldom compassion enough for the dulness of its owner to stay more than three days. Mr. Chillingly Mivers, indeed, had not exceeded that orthodox limit. Quietly observant, during his stay, of young Gordon's manner towards Cecilia, and hers towards him, he had satisfied himself that there was no cause to alarm Sir Peter or induce the worthy baronet to regret the invitation he had given to that clever kinsman. For all the visitors remaining, Exmundham had a charm.

To Lady Glenalvon, because in the hostess she met her most familiar friend when both were young girls, and because it pleased her to note the interest which Cecilia Travers took in the place so associated with memories of the man to whom it was Lady Glenalvon's hope to see her united. To Gordon Chillingly, because no opportunity could be so favourable for his own well-concealed designs on the hand and heart of the heiress. To the heiress herself the charm needs no explanation.

To Leopold Travers the attractions of Exmundham were unquestionably less fascinating. Still even he was well pleased to prolong his stay. His active mind found amusement in wandering over an estate the acreage of which would have warranted a much larger rental, and lecturing Sir Peter on the old-fashioned system of husbandry which that good-natured easy proprietor permitted his tenants to adopt, as well as on the number of superfluous hands that were employed on the pleasure grounds and in the general management of the estate, such as carpenters, sawyers, woodmen, bricklayers and smiths.

When the squire said, "You could do just as well with a third of those costly dependants." Sir

Peter, unconsciously plagiarizing the answer of the old French grand seigneur, replied, "Very likely. But the question is, could the rest do just as well without me?"

Exmundham, indeed, was a very expensive place to keep up. The house, built by some ambitious Chillingly three centuries ago, would have been large for an owner of thrice the revenues; and though the flower garden was smaller than that at Braefieldville, there were paths and drives through miles of young plantations and old woodlands that furnished lazy occupation to an army of labourers. No wonder that, despite his nominal ten thousand a year, Sir Peter was far from being a rich man. Exmundham devoured at least half the rental. The active mind of Leopold Travers also found ample occupation in the stores of his host's extensive library. Travers, never much of a reader, was by no means a despiser of learning, and he soon took to historical and archæological researches with the ardour of a man who must always throw energy into any pursuit that occasion presents as an escape from indolence,

Indolent, Leopold Travers never could be. But, more than either of these resources of occupation, the companionship of Chillingly Gordon excited his interest and quickened the current of his thoughts. Always fond of renewing his own youth in the society of the young, and of the sympathizing temperament which belongs to cordial natures, he had, as we have seen, entered very heartily into the ambition of George Belvoir, and reconciled himself very pliably to the humours of Kenelm Chillingly. But the first of these two was a little too commonplace, the second a little too eccentric, to enlist the complete good-fellowship which, being alike very clever and very practical, Leopold Travers established with that very clever and very practical representative of the rising generation, Chillingly Gordon. Between them there was this meeting-ground, political and worldly, a great contempt for innocuous old-fashioned notions; added to which, in the mind of Leopold Travers, was a contempt—which would have been complete, but that the contempt admitted dread—of harmful new-fashioned notions which, interpreted by his thoughts, threatened ruin to his country and downfall to the follies of existent society, and which, interpreted by his language, tamed itself into the man of the world's phrase, "Going too far for me." Notions which, by the much more cultivated intellect and the immeasurably more soaring ambition of Chillingly Gordon, might be viewed and criticized thus: "Could I accept these doctrines? I don't see my way to being Prime Minister of a country in which religion and capital are still powers to be consulted. And, putting aside religion and capital, I don't see how, if these doctrines passed into law, with a good coat on my back I should not be a sufferer. Either I, as having a good coat, should have it torn off my back as a capitalist, or, if I remonstrated in the name of moral honesty, be put to death as a religionist."

Therefore when Leopold Travers said "Of course we must go on," Chillingly Gordon smiled and answered, "Certainly, go on." And when Leopold Travers added, "But we may go too far," Chillingly Gordon shook his head, and replied, "How true that is! Certainly, too far."

Apart from the congeniality of political sentiment, there were other points of friendly contact between the older and younger man. Each was an exceedingly pleasant man of the world; and, though Leopold Travers could not have plumbed certain deeps in Chillingly Gordon's nature—and in every man's nature there are deeps which his ablest observer cannot fathom—yet he was not wrong when he said to himself, "Gordon is a gentleman."

Utterly would my readers misconceive that very clever young man, if they held him to be a hypocrite like Blifil or Joseph Surface. Chillingly Gordon, in every private sense of the word, was a gentleman. If he had staked his whole fortune on a rubber at whist, and an undetected glance at his adversary's hand would have made the difference between loss and gain, he would have turned away his head and said, "Hold up your cards." Neither, as I have had occasion to explain before, was he actuated by any motive in common with the vulgar fortune-hunter in his secret resolve to win the hand of the heiress. He recognized no inequality of worldly gifts between them. He said to himself, "Whatever she may give me in money, I shall amply repay in worldly position if I succeed, and succeed I certainly shall. If I were as rich as Lord Westminster, and still cared about being Prime Minister, I should select her as the most fitting woman I have seen for a Prime Minister's wife."

It must be acknowledged that this sort of self-commune, if not that of a very ardent lover, is very much that of a sensible man setting high value on himself, bent on achieving the prizes of a public career, and desirous of securing in his wife a woman who would adorn the station to which he confidently aspired. In fact, no one so able as Chillingly Gordon would ever have conceived the ambition of being Minister of England if, in all that, in private life, constitutes the English gentleman, he could be fairly subject to reproach.

He was but in public life what many a gentleman honest in private life has been before him, an ambitious, resolute egotist, by no means without personal affections, but holding them all subordinate to the objects of personal ambition, and with no more of other principle than that of expediency in reference to his own career, than would cover a silver penny. But expediency in itself he deemed the statesman's only rational principle. And to the consideration of expediency he brought a very unprejudiced intellect, quite fitted to decide whether the public opinion of a free and enlightened people was for turning St. Paul's Cathedral into an Agapemone or not.

During the summer weeks he had thus vouchsafed to the turfs and groves of Exmundham, Leopold Travers was not the only person whose good opinion Chillingly Gordon had ingratiated. He had won the warmest approbation from Mrs. Campion. His conversation reminded her of that which she had enjoyed in the house of her departed spouse. In talking with Cecilia she was fond of contrasting him to Kenelm, not to the favour of the latter, whose humours she utterly failed to understand, and whom she pertinaciously described as "So affected." "A most superior young man Mr. Gordon, so well informed, so sensible, above all, so natural." Such was her judgment upon the unavowed candidate to Cecilia's hand; and Mrs. Campion required no avowal to divine the candidature. Even Lady Glenalvon had begun to take friendly interest in the fortunes of this promising young man. Most women can sympathize with youthful ambition. He impressed her with a deep conviction of his abilities, and still more with respect for their concentration upon practical objects of power and renown. She too, like Mrs. Campion, began to draw comparisons unfavourable to Kenelm between the two cousins; the one who seemed so slothfully determined to hide his candle under a bushel, the other so honestly disposed to set his light before men. She felt also annoyed and angry that Kenelm was thus absenting himself from the paternal home at the very time of her first visit to it, and when he had so felicitous an opportunity of seeing more of the girl in whom he knew that Lady Glenalvon deemed he might win, if he would properly woo, the wife that would best suit him. So that when one day Mrs. Campion, walking through the gardens alone with Lady Glenalvon, while from the gardens into the park went Chillingly Gordon arm-in-arm with Leopold Travers, abruptly asked, "Don't you think that Mr. Gordon is smitten with Cecilia, though he, with his moderate fortune, does not dare to say so? And don't you think that any girl, if she were as rich as Cecilia will be, would be more proud of such a husband as Chillingly Gordon than of some silly Earl?"

Lady Glenalvon answered curtly, but somewhat sorrowfully—

"Yes."

After a pause, she added, "There *is* a man with whom I did once think she would have been happier than with any other. One man who ought to be dearer to me than Mr. Gordon, for he saved the life of my son, and who, though perhaps less clever than Mr. Gordon, still has a great deal of talent within him, which might come forth and make him—what shall I say?—a useful and distinguished member of society, if married to a girl so sure of raising any man she marries as Cecilia Travers. But if I am to renounce that hope, and look through the range of young men brought under my notice, I don't know one, putting aside consideration of rank and fortune, I should prefer for a clever daughter who went heart and soul with the ambition of a clever man. But, Mrs. Campion, I have not yet quite renounced my hope; and, unless I do, I yet think there is one man to whom I would rather give Cecilia, if she were my daughter."

Therewith Lady Glenalvon so decidedly broke off the subject of conversation, that Mrs. Campion could not have renewed it without such a breach of the female etiquette of good breeding as Mrs. Campion was the last person to adventure.

. Lady Chillingly could not help being pleased with Gordon. He was light in hand, served to amuse her guests, and made up a rubber of whist in case of need.

There were two persons, however, with whom Gordon made no ground, viz., Parson John and Sir Peter. When Travers praised him one day, for the solidity of his parts and the soundness of his judgment, the Parson replied snappishly, "Yes, solid and sound as one of those tables you buy at a broker's; the thickness of the varnish hides the defects in the joints; the whole framework is rickety." But when the Parson was indignantly urged to state the reason by which he arrived at so harsh a conclusion, he could only reply by an assertion which seemed to his questioner a declamatory burst of parsonic intolerance.

"Because," said Parson John, "he has no love for man, and no reverence for God. And no character is sound and solid which enlarges its surface at the expense of its supports."

On the other hand, the favour with which Sir Peter had at first regarded Gordon gradually vanished, in proportion as, acting on the hint Mivers had originally thrown out but did not deem it necessary to repeat, he watched the pains which the young man took to insinuate himself into the good graces of Mr. Travers and Mrs. Campion, and the artful and half-suppressed gallantry of his manner to the heiress.

Perhaps Gordon had not ventured thus "to feel his way" till after Mivers had departed; or perhaps Sir Peter's parental anxiety rendered him, in this instance, a shrewder observer than was the man of the world, whose natural acuteness was, in matters of affection, not unfrequently rendered languid by his acquired philosophy of indifferentism.

More and more every day, every hour, of her sojourn beneath his roof, did Cecilia become dearer to Sir Peter, and stronger and stronger became his wish to secure her for his daughter-in-law. He was inexpressibly flattered by her preference for his company; ever at hand to share his customary walks, his kindly visits to the cottages of peasants, or the homesteads of petty tenants; wherein both were sure to hear many a simple anecdote of Master Kenelm in his childhood, anecdotes of whim or good nature, of considerate pity or reckless courage.

Throughout all these varieties of thought or feeling in the social circle around her, Lady Chillingly preserved the unmoved calm of her dignified position. A very good woman certainly, and very ladylike. No one could detect a flaw in her character, or a fold awry in her flounce. She was only, like the gods of Epicurus, too good to trouble her serene existence with the cares of us simple mortals. Not that she was without a placid satisfaction in the tribute which the world laid upon her altars; nor was she so supremely goddess-like as to soar above the household affections which humanity entails on the dwellers and denizens of earth. She liked her husband as much as most elderly wives like their elderly husbands. She bestowed upon Kenelm a liking somewhat more warm, and mingled with compassion. His eccentricities would have puzzled her, if she had allowed herself to be puzzled; it troubled her less to pity them. She did not share her husband's desire for his union with

Cecilia. She thought that her son would have a higher place in the county if he married Lady Jane, the Duke of Clanville's daughter; and "that is what he ought to do," said Lady Chillingly to herself. She entertained none of the fear that had induced Sir Peter to extract from Kenelm the promise not to pledge his hand before he had received his father's consent. That the son of Lady Chillingly should make a *misalliance*, however crotchety he might be in other respects, was a thought that it would have so disturbed her to admit, that she did not admit it.

Such was the condition of things at Exmundham, when the lengthy communication of Kenelm reached Sir Peter's hands.

BOOK VIII.

CHAPTER I.

NEVER in his whole life had the mind of Sir Peter been so agitated as it was during, and after, the perusal of Kenelm's flighty composition. He had received it at the breakfast table, and, opening it eagerly, ran his eye hastily over the contents, till he very soon arrived at sentences which appalled him. Lady Chillingly, who was fortunately busied at the tea urn, did not observe the dismay on his countenance. It was visible only to Cecilia and to Gordon. Neither guessed who that letter was from.

"Not bad news, I hope," said Cecilia softly.

"Bad news," echoed Sir Peter. "No, my dear, no; a letter on business. It seems terribly long," and he thrust the packet into his pocket, muttering, "see to it by-and-by."

"That slovenly farmer of yours, Mr. Nostock,

has failed, I suppose," said Mr. Travers, looking up and observing a quiver on his host's lip. "I told you he would—a fine farm too. Let me choose you another tenant."

Sir Peter shook his head with a wan smile.

"Nostock will not fail. There have been six generations of Nostocks on the farm."

"So I should guess," said Travers drily.

"And—and," faltered Sir Peter, "if the last of the race fails, he must lean upon me, and—if one of the two break down—it shall not be—"

"Shall not be that cross-cropping blockhead, my dear Sir Peter. This is carrying benevolence too far."

Here the tact and *savoir vivre* of Chillingly Gordon came to the rescue of the host. Possessing himself of the *Times* newspaper, he uttered an exclamation of surprise, genuine or simulated, and read aloud an extract from the leading article, announcing an impending change in the Cabinet.

As soon as he could quit the breakfast-table, Sir Peter hurried into his library, and there gave himself up to the study of Kenelm's unwelcome communication. The task took him long, for he stopped at intervals, overcome by the struggle of his heart, now melted into sympathy with the passionate eloquence of a son hitherto so free from amorous romance, and now sorrowing for the ruin of his own cherished hopes. This uneducated country girl would never be such a helpmate to a man like Kenelm as would have been Cecilia Travers. At length, having finished the letter, he buried his head between his clasped hands, and tried hard to realize the situation that placed the father and son into such direct antagonism.

"But," he murmured, "after all it is the boy's happiness that must be consulted. If he will not be happy in my way, what right have I to say that he shall not be happy in his?"

Just then Cecilia came softly into the room. She had acquired the privilege of entering his library at will, sometimes to choose a book of his recommendation, sometimes to direct and seal his letters—Sir Peter was grateful to any one who saved him an extra trouble—and sometimes, especially at this hour, to decoy him forth into his wonted constitutional walk.

He lifted his face at the sound of her approaching tread and her winning voice, and the face was so sad that the tears rushed to her eyes on seeing it. She laid her hand on his shoulder, and said pleadingly, "Dear Sir Peter, what is it—what is it?"

"Ah—ah, my dear," said Sir Peter, gathering up the scattered sheets of Kenelm's effusion with hurried, trembling hands. "Don't ask—don't talk of it; 'tis but one of the disappointments that all of us must undergo, when we invest our hopes in the uncertain will of others."

Then, observing that the tears were trickling down the girl's fair, pale cheeks, he took her hand in both his, kissed her forehead, and said, whisperingly, "Pretty one, how good you have been to me! Heaven bless you. What a wife you will be to some man!"

Thus saying, he shambled out of the room through the open casement. She followed him impulsively, wonderingly; but before she reached his side he turned round, waved his hand with a gently repelling gesture, and went his way alone through dense fir groves which had been planted in honour of Kenelm's birth.

CHAPTER II.

KENELM arrived at Exmundham just in time to dress for dinner. His arrival was not unexpected, for the morning after his father had received his communication, Sir Peter had said to Lady Chillingly "that he had heard from Kenelm to the effect that he might be down any day."

"Quite time he should come," said Lady Chillingly. "Have you his letter about you?"

"No, my dear Caroline. Of course he sends you his kindest love, poor fellow."

"Why poor fellow? Has he been ill?"

"No; but there seems to be something on his mind. If so, we must do what we can to relieve it. He is the best of sons, Caroline."

"I am sure I have nothing to say against him, except," added her ladyship reflectively "that I do wish he were a little more like other young men."

"Hum—like Chillingly Gordon, for instance?"

"Well, yes; Mr. Gordon is a remarkably well-bred, sensible young man. How different from that disagreeable, bearish father of his, who went to law with you!"

"Very different indeed, but with just as much of the Chillingly blood in him. How the Chillinglys ever gave birth to a Kenelm is a question much more puzzling."

"Oh, my dear Sir Peter, don't be metaphysical. You know how I hate puzzles."

"And yet, Caroline, I have to thank you for a puzzle which I can never interpret by my brain. There are a great many puzzles in human nature which can only be interpreted by the heart."

"Very true," said Lady Chillingly. "I suppose Kenelm is to have his old room, just opposite to Mr. Gordon's."

"Ay—ay, just opposite. Opposite they will be all their lives. Only think, Caroline, I have made a discovery."

"Dear me; I hope not. Your discoveries are

generally very expensive, and bring us in contact with such very odd people."

"This discovery shall not cost us a penny, and I don't know any people so odd as not to comprehend it. Briefly it is this: To genius the first requisite is heart; it is no requisite at all to talent. My dear Caroline, Gordon has as much talent as any young man I know, but he wants the first requisite of genius. I am not by any means sure that Kenelm has genius, but there is no doubt that he has the first requisite of genius —heart. Heart is a very perplexing, wayward, irrational thing; and that perhaps accounts for the general incapacity to comprehend genius, while any fool can comprehend talent. My dear Caroline, you know that it is very seldom, not more than once in three years, that I presume to have a will of my own against a will of yours; but should there come a question in which our son's heart is concerned, then (speaking between ourselves) my will must govern yours."

"Sir Peter is growing more odd every day," said Lady Chillingly to herself when left alone.

"But he does not mean ill, and there are worse husbands in the world."

Therewith she rang for her maid, gave requisite orders for the preparing of Kenelm's room, which had not been slept in for many months, and then consulted that functionary as to the adaptation of some dress of hers, too costly to be laid aside, to the style of some dress less costly which Lady Glenalvon had imported from Paris as *la dernière mode*.

On the very day on which Kenelm arrived at Exmundham, Chillingly Gordon had received this letter from Mr. Gerard Danvers:

"DEAR GORDON,—In the ministerial changes announced as rumour in the public papers, and which you may accept as certain, that sweet little cherub * * * is to be sent to sit up aloft and pray there for the life of poor Jack—viz., of the government he leaves below. In accepting the peerage, which I persuaded him to do * * * creates a vacancy for the borough of —— just the place for you, far better in every way than

Saxborough. * * * promises to recommend you to his committee. Come to town at once.

"Yours, &c.

"G. Danvers."

Gordon shewed this letter to Mr. Travers, and, on receiving the hearty good wishes of that gentleman, said, with emotion partly genuine partly assumed, "You cannot guess all that the realization of your good wishes would be. Once in the House of Commons, and my motives for action are so strong that—do not think me very conceited if I count upon Parliamentary success."

"My dear Gordon, I am as certain of your success as I am of my own existence."

"Should I succeed—should the great prizes of public life be within my reach—should I lift myself into a position that would warrant my presumption, do you think I could come to you and say, 'There is an object of ambition, dearer to me than power and office—the hope of attaining which was the strongest of all my motives of action? And in that hope shall I also have the good wishes of the father of Cecilia Travers?'"

"My dear fellow, give me your hand; you speak manfully and candidly as a gentleman should speak. I answer in the same spirit. I don't pretend to say that I have not entertained views for Cecilia which included hereditary rank and established fortune in a suitor to her hand, though I never should have made them imperative conditions. I am neither potentate nor *parvenu* enough for that; and I can never forget" (here every muscle in the man's face twitched) "that I myself married for love, and was so happy. How happy Heaven only knows! Still, if you had thus spoken a few weeks ago, I should not have replied very favourably to your question. But now that I have seen so much of you, my answer is this: If you lose your election—if you don't come into Parliament at all, you have my good wishes all the same. If you win my daughter's heart, there is no man on whom I would more willingly bestow her hand. There she is, by herself too, in the garden. Go and talk to her."

Gordon hesitated. He knew too well that he had not won her heart, though he had no suspicion that it was given to another. And he was much too clever not to know also how much he hazards, who, in affairs of courtship, is premature.

"Ah!" he said, "I cannot express my gratitude for words so generous, encouragement so cheering. But I have never yet dared to utter to Miss Travers a word that would prepare her even to harbour a thought of me as a suitor. And I scarcely think I should have the courage to go through this election with the grief of her rejection on my heart."

"Well, go in and win the election first; meanwhile, at all events, take leave of Cecilia."

Gordon left his friend, and joined Miss Travers, resolved not indeed to risk a formal declaration, but to sound his way to his chances of acceptance.

The interview was very brief. He did sound his way skilfully, and felt it very unsafe for his footsteps. The advantage of having gained the approval of the father was too great to be lost altogether, by one of these decided answers on the part of the daughter which allow of no appeal, especially to a poor gentleman who woos an heiress.

He returned to Travers, and said simply, "I bear with me her good wishes as well as yours. That is all. I leave myself in your kind hands."

Then he hurried away to take leave of his host and hostess, say a few significant words to the ally he had already gained in Mrs. Campion, and within an hour was on his road to London, passing on his way the train that bore Kenelm to Exmundham. Gordon was in high spirits. At least he felt as certain of winning Cecilia as he did of winning his election.

"I have never yet failed in what I desired," said he to himself, "because I have ever taken pains not to fail."

The cause of Gordon's sudden departure created a great excitement in that quiet circle, shared by all except Cecilia and Sir Peter.

CHAPTER III.

KENELM did not see either father or mother till he appeared at dinner. Then he was seated next to Cecilia. There was but little conversation between the two; in fact, the prevalent subject of talk was general and engrossing, the interest in Chillingly Gordon's election; predictions of his success, of what he would do in Parliament. "Where," said Lady Glenalvon, "there is such a dearth of rising young men, that if he were only half as clever as he is he would be a gain."

"A gain to what?" asked Sir Peter testily. "To his country? about which I don't believe he cares a brass button."

To this assertion Leopold Travers replied warmly, and was not less warmly backed by Mrs. Campion.

"For my part," said Lady Glenalvon, in conciliatory accents, "I think every able man in Parliament is a gain to the country; and he may not serve his country less effectively because he does not boast of his love for it. The politicians I dread most are those so rampant in France now-a-days, the bawling patriots. When Sir Robert Walpole said, 'All those men have their price,' he pointed to the men who called themselves 'patriots.'"

"Bravo!" cried Travers.

"Sir Robert Walpole showed his love for his country by corrupting it. There are many ways besides bribing for corrupting a country," said Kenelm mildly, and that was Kenelm's sole contribution to the general conversation.

It was not till the rest of the party had retired to rest, that the conference, longed for by Kenelm, dreaded by Sir Peter, took place in the library. It lasted deep into the night; both parted with lightened hearts and a fonder affection for each other. Kenelm had drawn so charming a picture of the Fairy, and so thoroughly convinced Sir Peter that his own feelings towards her were those of no passing youthful fancy, but of that love which has its roots in the innermost heart, that though it was still with a sigh, a deep sigh, that he dismissed the thought of Cecilia, Sir Peter did dismiss it; and, taking comfort at last from the positive assurance that Lily was of gentle birth, and the fact that her name of Mordaunt was that of ancient and illustrious houses, said, with half a smile, "It might have been worse, my dear boy. I began to be afraid that, in spite of the teachings of Mivers and Welby, it was 'The Miller's Daughter,' after all. But we still have a difficult task to persuade your poor mother. In covering your first flight from our roof I unluckily put into her head the notion of Lady Jane, a duke's daughter, and the notion has never got out of it. That comes of fibbing."

"I count on Lady Glenalvon's influence on my mother in support of your own," said Kenelm. "If so accepted an oracle in the great world pronounce in my favour, and promise to present my wife at Court and bring her into fashion, I think that my mother will consent to allow us to reset the old family diamonds for her next re-appearance in London. And then, too, you can tell her that I will stand for the county. I will go into Parliament, and if I meet there our clever cousin, and find that he does not care a brass button for the country, take my word for it, I will lick him more easily than I licked Tom Bowles."

"Tom Bowles! Who is he?—ah! I remember some letter of yours in which you spoke of a Bowles, whose favourite study was mankind, a moral philosopher."

"Moral philosophers," answered Kenelm, "have so muddled their brains with the alcohol of new ideas that their moral legs have become shaky, and the humane would rather help them to bed than give them a licking. My Tom Bowles in a muscular Christian, who became no less muscular, but much more Christian, after he was licked."

And in this pleasant manner these two oddities settled their conference, and went up to bed with arms wrapt round each other's shoulder.

CHAPTER IV.

KENELM found it a much harder matter to win Lady Glenalvon to his side than he had anticipated. With the strong interest she had taken in Kenelm's future, she could not but revolt from the idea of his union with an obscure portionless girl whom he had only known a few weeks, and of whose very parentage he seemed to know nothing, save an assurance that she was his equal in birth. And, with the desire, which she had cherished almost as fondly as Sir Peter, that Kenelm might win a bride in every way so worthy of his choice as Cecilia Travers, she felt not less indignant than regretful at the overthrow of her plans.

At first, indeed, she was so provoked that she would not listen to his pleadings. She broke away from him with a rudeness she had never exhibited to any one before, refused to grant him another interview in order to re-discuss the matter, and said that so far from using her influence in favour of his romantic folly, she would remonstrate well with Lady Chillingly and Sir Peter against yielding their assent to his "thus throwing himself away."

It was not till the third day after his arrival that, touched by the grave but haughty mournfulness of his countenance, she yielded to the arguments of Sir Peter in the course of a private conversation with that worthy baronet. Still it was reluctantly (she did not fulfil her threat of remonstrance with Lady Chillingly) that she conceded the point, that a son who, succeeding to the absolute fee simple of an estate, had volunteered the resettlement of it on terms singularly generous to both his parents, was entitled to some sacrifice of their inclinations on a question in which he deemed his happiness vitally concerned; and that he was of age to choose for himself, independently of their consent, but for a previous promise extracted from him by his father, a promise which, rigidly construed, was not extended to Lady Chillingly, but confined to Sir Peter as the head of the family and master of the household. The father's consent was already given, and, if in his reverence for both parents Kenelm could not dispense with his mother's approval, surely it was the part of a true friend to remove every scruple from his conscience, and smooth away every obstacle to a love not to be condemned because it was disinterested.

After this conversation Lady Glenalvon sought Kenelm, found him gloomily musing on the banks of the trout stream, took his arm, led him into the sombre glades of the fir grove, and listened patiently to all he had to say. Even then her woman's heart was not won to his reasonings, until he said pathetically, "You thanked me once for saving your son's life; you said then that you could never repay me; you can repay me tenfold. Could your son who is now, we trust, in heaven, look down and judge between us, do you think he would approve you if you refuse?"

Then Lady Glenalvon wept, and took his hand, kissed his forehead as a mother might kiss it, and said, "You triumph, I will go to Lady Chillingly at once. Marry her whom you so love, on one condition; marry her from my house."

Lady Glenalvon was not one of those women who serve a friend by halves. She knew well how to propitiate and reason down the apathetic temperament of Lady Chillingly; she did not cease till that lady herself came into Kenelm's room, and said very quietly,

"So you are going to propose to Miss Mordaunt, the Warwickshire Mordaunts I suppose. Lady Glenalvon says she is a very lovely girl, and will stay with her before the wedding. And, as the young lady is an orphan, Lady Glenalvon's uncle the Duke, who is connected with the eldest branch of the Mordaunts, will give her away. It will be a very brilliant affair. I am sure I wish you happy, it is time you should have sown your wild oats."

Two days after the consent thus formally given, Kenelm quitted Exmundham. Sir Peter would have accompanied him to pay his respects to the intended, but the agitation he had gone through brought on a sharp twinge of the gout, which consigned his feet to flannels.

After Kenelm had gone, Lady Glenalvon went into Cecilia's room. Cecilia was seated very desolately by the open window; she had detected that something of an anxious and painful nature had been weighing upon the minds of father and son, and had connected it with the letter which had so disturbed the even mind of Sir Peter; but she did not divine what the something was, and if mortified by a certain reserve, more distant than heretofore, which had characterized Kenelm's manner towards herself, the mortification was less sensibly felt than a tender sympathy for the sadness she had observed on his face, and yearned to soothe. His reserve had, however, made her own manner more reserved than of old, for which she was now rather chiding herself than reproaching him.

Lady Glenalvon put her arms round Cecilia's neck and kissed her, whispering, "That man has so disappointed me, he is so unworthy of the happiness I had once hoped for him!"

"Whom do you speak of?" murmured Cecilia, turning very pale.

"Kenelm Chillingly. It seems that he has conceived a fancy for some penniless girl whom he has met in his wanderings, has come here to get the consent of his parents to propose to her, has obtained their consent, and is gone to propose."

Cecilia remained silent for a moment with her eyes closed, then she said, "He is worthy of all happiness, and he would never make an unworthy choice. Heaven bless him—and—and—" She would have added "his bride," but her lips refused to utter the word bride.

"Cousin Gordon is worth ten of him," cried Lady Glenalvon indignantly.

She had served Kenelm, but she had not forgiven him.

CHAPTER V.

KENELM slept in London that night, and, the next day being singularly fine for an English summer, he resolved to go to Moleswick on foot. He had no need this time to encumber himself with a knapsack; he had left sufficient change of dress in his lodgings at Cromwell Lodge.

It was towards the evening when he found himself in one of the prettiest rural villages by which

> "Wanders the hoary Thames along
> His silver-winding way."

It was not in the direct road from London to Moleswick, but it was a pleasanter way for a pedestrian. And when, quitting the long street of the sultry village, he came to the shelving margin of the river, he was glad to rest awhile, enjoy the cool of the rippling waters, and listen to their placid murmurs amid the rushes in the bordering shallows. He had ample time before him. His rambles while at Cromwell Lodge had made him familiar with the district for miles round Moleswick, and he knew that a footpath through the fields at the right would lead him, in less than an hour, to the side of the tributary brook on which Cromwell Lodge was placed, opposite the wooden bridge which conducted to Grasmere and Moleswick.

To one who loves the romance of history, English history, the whole course of the Thames is full of charm. Ah! could I go back to the days in which younger generations than that of Kenelm Chillingly were unborn, when every wave of the Rhine spoke of history and romance to me, what fairies should meet on thy banks, O thou, our own Father Thames! Perhaps some day a German pilgrim may repay tenfold to thee the tribute rendered by the English kinsman to the Father Rhine.

Listening to the whispers of the reeds, Kenelm Chillingly felt the haunting influence of the legendary stream. Many a poetic incident or tradition in antique chronicle, many a votive rhyme in song, dear to forefathers whose very names have become a poetry to us, thronged dimly and confusedly back to his memory, which had little cared to retain such graceful trinkets in the treasure-house of love. But everything that, from childhood upward, connects itself with romance—revives with yet fresher bloom in the memories of him who loves.

And to this man, through the first perilous season of youth, so abnormally safe from youth's most wonted peril,—to this would-be pupil of realism, this learned adept in the schools of a Welby or a Mivers,—to this man, Love came at last as with the fatal powers of the fabled Cytherèa; and with that love all the realisms of life became ideals, all the stern lines of our commonplace destinies undulating into curves of beauty, all the trite sounds of our everyday life attuned into delicacies of song. How full of sanguine yet dreamy bliss was his heart,—and seemed his future,—in the gentle breeze and the softened glow of that summer eve! He should see Lily the next morn, and his lips were now free to say all that they had as yet suppressed.

Suddenly he was roused from the half-awake, half-asleep, happiness that belongs to the moments in which we transport ourselves into Elysium, by the carol of a voice more loudly joyous than that of his own heart—

> "Singing—singing,
> Lustily singing,
> Down the road, with his dogs before,
> Came the Ritter of Nierestein."

Kenelm turned his head so quickly that he frightened Max, who had for the last minute been standing behind him inquisitively with one paw raised, and sniffing, in some doubt whether he recognized an old acquaintance; but at Kenelm's quick movement the animal broke into a nervous bark, and ran back to his master.

The Minstrel, little heeding the figure reclined on the bank, would have passed on with his light tread and his cheery carol, but Kenelm rose to his feet, and holding out his hand, said, "I hope you don't share Max's alarm at meeting me again?"

"Ah, my young philosopher, is it indeed you?"

"If I am to be designated a philosopher it is certainly not I. And, honestly speaking, I am not the same. I, who spent that pleasant day with you among the fields round Luscombe two years ago"—

"Or who advised me at Tor Hadham to string my lyre to the praise of a beefsteak. I too am not quite the same, I whose dog presented you with the begging-tray."

"Yet you still go through the world singing."

"Even that vagrant singing time is pretty well over. But I disturbed you from your repose. I would rather share it; you are probably not going my way, and as I am in no hurry, I should not like to lose the opportunity chance has so happily given me of renewing acquaintance with one who has often been present to my thoughts since we last met." Thus saying, the Minstrel stretched himself at ease on the bank, and Kenelm followed his example.

There certainly was a change in the owner of the dog with the begging tray, a change in costume in countenance, in that indescribable self-evidence which we call "manner." The costume was not that Bohemian attire in which Kenelm had first encountered the Wandering Minstrel, nor the studied, more graceful garb, which so well became his shapely form, during his visit to Luscombe. It was now neatly simple, the cool and quiet summer dress any English gentleman might adopt in a long rural walk. And as he uncovered his head to court the cooling breeze, there was a graver dignity in the man's handsome Rubens-like face, a line of more concentrated thought in the spacious forehead, a thread or two of grey shimmering here and there through the thick auburn curls of hair and beard. And in his manner, though still very frank, there was just perceptible a sort of self-assertion, not offensive, but manly; such as does not misbecome one of maturer years, and of some established position, addressing another man much younger than himself, who in all probability has achieved no position at all beyond that which the accident of birth might assign to him.

"Yes," said the Minstrel, with a half-suppressed sigh, "the last year of my vagrant holidays has come to its close. I recollect that the first day we met by the roadside fountain, I advised you to do like me, seek amusement and adventure as a foot traveller. Now, seeing you, evidently a gentleman by education and birth, still a foot traveller, I feel as if I ought to say, 'You have had enough of such experience; vagabond life has its perils as well as charms; cease it and settle down.'"

"I think of doing so," replied Kenelm laconically.

"In a profession?—army—law—medicine?"

"No."

"Ah, in marriage then. Right; give me your hand on that. So a petticoat indeed has at last found its charm for you in the actual world as well as on the canvas of a picture?"

"I conclude," said Kenelm,—evading any direct notice of that playful taunt,—"I conclude from your remark that it is in marriage *you* are about to settle down."

"Ay, could I have done so before I should have been saved from many errors, and been many years nearer to the goal which dazzled my sight through the haze of my boyish dreams."

"What is that goal—the grave?"

"The grave! That which allows of no grave—Fame."

"I see, despite of what you just now said—you still mean to go through the world seeking a poet's fame."

"Alas! I resign that fancy," said the Minstrel, with another half sigh. "It was not indeed wholly, but in great part the hope of the poet's fame that made me a truant in the way to that which destiny and such few gifts as nature conceded to me, marked out for my proper and only goal. But what a strange, delusive Will-o'-the-Wisp the love of verse-making is! How rarely a man of good sense deceives himself as to other things for which he is fitted, in which he can succeed; but let him once drink into his being the charm of verse-making, how the glamour of the charm bewitches his understanding! how long it is before he can believe that the world will not take his word for it, when he cries out to sun, moon, and stars, 'I, too, am a poet.' And with what agonies, as if at the wrench of soul from life, he resigns himself at last to the conviction, that whether he or the world be right, it comes to the same thing. Who can plead his cause before a court that will not give him a hearing?"

It was with an emotion so passionately strong, and so intensely painful, that the owner of the dog with the begging-tray thus spoke, that Kenelm felt, through sympathy, as if he himself were torn asunder by the wrench of life from soul. But then, Kenelm was a mortal so eccentric, that, if a single acute suffering endured by a fellow-mortal could be brought before the evidence of his senses, I doubt whether he would not have suffered as much as that fellow-mortal. So that, though if there were a thing in the world which Kenelm Chillingly would care not to do, it was verse-making, his mind involuntarily hastened to the arguments by which he could best mitigate the pang of the verse-maker.

Quoth he—"According to my very scanty reading, you share the love of verse-making with men the most illustrious in careers which have achieved the goal of fame. It must, then, be a very noble love — Augustus, Pollio, Varius, Mæcenas—the greatest statesmen of their day; they were verse-makers. Cardinal Richelieu was a verse-maker; Walter Raleigh and Philip Sidney; Fox, Burke, Sheridan, Warren Hastings, Canning —even the grave William Pitt; all were verse-makers. Verse-making did not retard—no doubt the qualities essential to verse-making accelerated —their race to the goal of fame. What great painters have been verse-makers! Michael Angelo, Leonardo da Vinci, Salvator Rosa"—and Heaven knows how many other great names Kenelm Chillingly might have proceeded to add to his list, if the Minstrel had not here interposed.

"What! all those mighty painters were verse-makers?"

"Verse-makers so good, especially Michael Angelo—the greatest painter of all—that they would have had the fame of poets, if, unfortunately for that goal of fame, their glory in the sister art of painting did not outshine it. But, when you give to your gift of song the modest title of verse-making, permit me to observe that your gift is perfectly distinct from that of the verse-maker. Your gift, whatever it may be, could not exist without some sympathy with the nonverse-making human heart. No doubt, in your foot travels, you have acquired not only observant intimacy with external nature in the shifting hues at each hour of a distant mountain, in the lengthening shadows which yon sunset casts on the waters at our feet, in the habits of the thrush dropped fearlessly close beside me, in that turf moistened by its neighbourhood to those dripping rushes, all of which I could describe no less accurately than you—as a Peter Bell might describe them no less accurately than a William Wordsworth. But in such songs of yours as you have permitted me to hear, you seem to have escaped out of that elementary accidence of the poet's art, and to touch, no matter how slightly, on the only lasting interest which the universal heart of man can have in the song of the poet, viz., in the sound which the poet's individual sympathy draws forth from the latent chords in that universal heart. As for what you call 'the world,' what is it more than the fashion of the present day? How far the judgment of that is worth a poet's pain I can't pretend to say. But of one thing I am sure, that while I could as easily square the circle as compose a simple couplet addressed to the heart of a simple audience with sufficient felicity to decoy their praises into Max's begging-tray, I could spin out by the yard the sort of verse-making which characterizes the fashion of the present day."

Much flattered, and not a little amused, the Wandering Minstrel turned his bright countenance, no longer dimmed by a cloud, towards that of his lazily reclined consoler, and answered gaily:

"You say that you could spin out by the

yard verses in the fashion of the present day. I wish you would give me a specimen of your skill in that handiwork."

"Very well; on one condition, that you will repay my trouble by a specimen of your own verses, not in the fashion of the present day,— something which I can construe. I defy you to construe mine."

"Agreed."

"Well then, let us take it for granted that this is the Augustan age of English poetry, and that the English language is dead, like the Latin. Suppose I am writing for a prize medal, in English, as I wrote at college for a prize medal, in Latin; of course, I shall be successful in proportion as I introduce the verbal elegances peculiar to our Augustan age, and also catch the prevailing poetic characteristic of that classical epoch.

"Now I think that every observant critic will admit that the striking distinctions of the poetry most in the fashion of the present day, viz., of the Augustan age, are—first, a selection of such verbal elegances as would have been most repulsive to the barbaric taste of the preceding century, and—secondly, a very lofty disdain of all prosaic condescensions to common sense, and an elaborate cultivation of that element of the sublime which Mr. Burke defines under the head of obscurity.

"These premises conceded, I will only ask you to choose the metre. Blank verse is very much in fashion just now."

"Pooh,—blank verse indeed—I am not going so to free your experiment from the difficulties of rhyme."

"It is all one to me," said Kenelm, yawning. "Rhyme be it: Heroic, or lyrical?"

"Heroics are old-fashioned; but the Chaucer couplet, as brought to perfection by our modern poets, I think the best adapted to dainty leaves and uncrackable nuts. I accept the modern Chaucerian."

"The subject?"

"Oh, never trouble yourself about that. By whatever title your Augustan verse-maker labels his poem, his genius, like Pindar's, disdains to be cramped by the subject. Listen, and don't suffer Max to howl, if he can help it. Here goes."

And in an affected, but emphatic, sing-song, Kenelm began—

> "In Attica the gentle Pythias dwelt.
> Youthful he was, and passing rich: he felt
> As if nor youth nor riches could suffice
> For bliss. Dark-eyed Sophronia was a nice
> Girl: and one summer day, when Neptune drove
> His sea-car slowly, and the olive grove love
> That skirts Ilissus, to thy shell, Harmonia,
> Rippled, he said 'I love thee' to Sophronia.
> Crocus and iris, when they heard him, wagg'd
> Their pretty heads in glee: the honey-bagg'd
> Bees became altars: and the forest dove
> Her plumage smooth'd. Such is the charm of love.
> Of this sweet story do ye long for more?
> Wait till I publish it in volumes four;
> Which certain critics, my good friends, will cry
> Up beyond Chaucer. Take their word for't. I
> Say 'Trust them: but not read,—or you'll not buy.'"

"You have certainly kept your word," said the Minstrel laughing. "And if this be the Augustan age, and the English were a dead language, you deserve to win the prize medal."

"You flatter me," said Kenelm modestly. "But if I, who never before strung two rhymes together, can improvise so readily in the style of the present day, why should not a practical rhymester like yourself dash off at a sitting a volume or so in the same style; disguising completely the verbal elegances borrowed, adding to the delicacies of the rhyme by the frequent introduction of a line that will not scan, and towering yet more into the sublime by becoming yet more unintelligible. Do that, and I promise you the most glowing panegyric in 'The Londoner,' for I will write it myself."

"'The Londoner!'" exclaimed the Minstrel, with an angry flush on his cheek and brow. "My bitter, relentless enemy."

"I fear, then, you have as little studied the critical press of the Augustan age as you have imbued your Muse with the classical spirit of its verse. For the art of writing a man must cultivate himself. The art of being reviewed consists in cultivating the acquaintance of reviewers. In the Augustan age criticism is cliquism. Belong to a clique, and you are Horace or Tibullus. Belong to no clique, and, of course, you are Bavius or Mævius. 'The Londoner' is the enemy of no man—it holds all men in equal contempt. But as, in order to amuse, it must abuse, it compensates the praise it is compelled to bestow upon the members of its clique by heaping additional scorn upon all who are cliqueless. Hit him hard, he has no friends."

"Ah," said the Minstrel, "I believe that there is much truth in what you say. I never had a friend among the cliques. And Heaven knows with what pertinacity those from whom I, in utter ignorance of the rules which govern the so-called organs of opinion, had hoped, in my time of struggle, for a little sympathy,—a kindly encouragement,—have combined to crush me down. They succeeded long. But at last I venture to hope that I am beating them. Happily, Nature endowed me with a sanguine, joyous, elastic temperament. He who never despairs seldom completely fails."

This speech rather perplexed Kenelm, for had not the Minstrel declared that his singing days were over, that he had decided on the renunciation of verse-making? What other path to fame, from which the critics had not been able to exclude his steps, was he, then, now pursuing? he whom Kenelm had assumed to belong to some commercial money-making firm. No doubt some less difficult prose-track; probably a novel. Everybody writes novels now-a-days, and as the public will read novels without being told to do so, and will not read poetry unless they are told that they ought, possibly novels are not quite so much at the mercy of cliques, as are the poems of our Augustan age.

However, Kenelm did not think of seeking for further confidence on that score. His mind at that moment, not unnaturally, wandered from books and critics to love and wedlock.

"Our talk," said he, "has digressed into fretful courses—permit me to return to the starting-point. You are going to settle down into the peace of home. A peaceful home is like a good conscience. The rains without do not pierce its roof, the winds without do not shake its walls. If not an impertinent question, is it long since you have known your intended bride?"

"Yes, very long."

"And always loved her?"

"Always, from her infancy. Out of all womankind, she was designed to be my life's playmate, and my soul's purifier. I know not what might have become of me, if the thought of her had not walked beside me, as my guardian angel. For, like many vagrants from the beaten highroads of the world, there is in my nature something of that lawlessness which belongs to high animal spirits, to the zest of adventure, and the warm blood which runs into song, chiefly because song is the voice of a joy. And, no doubt, when I look back on the past years I must own that I have too often been led astray from the objects set before my reason, and cherished at my heart, by erring impulse or wanton fancy."

"Petticoat interest, I presume," interposed Kenelm drily.

"I wish I could honestly answer 'No,'" said the Minstrel, colouring high. "But from the worst, from all that would have permanently blasted the career to which I intrust my fortunes, all that would have rendered me unworthy of the pure love that now, I trust, awaits and crowns my dreams of happiness, I have been saved by the haunting smile in a sinless infantine face. Only once was I in great peril—that hour of peril I recall with a shudder. It was at Luscombe."

"At Luscombe!"

"In the temptation of a terrible crime I thought I heard a voice say: 'Mischief! Remember the little child.' In that supervention which is so readily accepted as a divine warning, when the imagination is morbidly excited, and when the conscience, though lulled asleep for a moment, is still asleep so lightly that the sigh of a breeze, the fall of a leaf, can awake it with a start of terror, I took the voice for that of my guardian angel. Thinking over it later, and coupling the voice with the moral of those weird lines you repeated to me so appositely the next day, I conclude that I am not mistaken when I say it was from your lips that the voice which preserved me came."

"I confess the impertinence—you pardon it!"

The Minstrel seized Kenelm's hand and pressed it earnestly.

"Pardon it! Oh, could you but guess what cause I have to be grateful, everlastingly grateful! That sudden cry, the remorse and horror of my own self that it struck into me—deepened by those rugged lines which the next day made me shrink in dismay from 'the face of my darling sin'! Then came the turning-point of my life. From that day, the lawless vagabond within me was killed. I mean not, indeed, the love of nature and of song which had first allured the vagabond, but the hatred of steadfast habits and of serious work—*that* was killed. I no longer trifled with my calling, I took to it as a serious duty. And when I saw her, whom Fate has reserved and reared for my bride, her face was no longer in my eyes that of the playful child; the soul of the woman was dawning into it. It is but two years since that day, to me so eventful. Yet my fortunes are now secured. And if fame be not established, I am at last in a position which warrants my saying to her I love, 'The time has come when, without fear for thy future, I can ask thee to be mine.'"

The man spoke with so fervent a passion that Kenelm silently left him to recover his wonted self-possession,—not unwilling to be silent—not unwilling, in the softness of the hour, passing from roseate sunset into starry twilight, to murmur to himself, "And the time, too, has come for me!"

After a few moments the Minstrel resumed lightly and cheerily:

"Sir, your turn—pray have you long known —judging by our former conversation, you cannot have long loved—the lady whom you have wooed and won?"

As Kenelm had neither as yet wooed nor won the lady in question, and did not deem it necessary to enter into any details on the subject of love particular to himself, he replied by a general observation—

"It seems to me that the coming of love is like the coming of spring—the date is not to be reckoned by the calendar. It may be slow and gradual; it may be quick and sudden. But in the morning, when we wake and recognize a change in the world without, verdure on the trees, blossoms on the sward, warmth in the sunshine, music in the air, then we say Spring has come!"

"I like your illustration. And if it be an idle question to ask a lover how long he has known the beloved one, so it is almost as idle to ask if she be not beautiful. He cannot but see in her face the beauty she has given to the world without."

"True; and that thought is poetic enough to make me remind you that I favoured you with the maiden specimen of my verse-making on condition that you repaid me by a specimen of your own practical skill in the art. And I claim the right to suggest the theme. Let it be——"

"Of a beef-steak?"

"Tush, you have worn out that tasteless joke

at my expense. The theme must be of love, and if you could improvise a stanza or two expressive of the idea you just uttered I shall listen with yet more pleased attention."

"Alas! I am no improvisatore. Yet I will avenge myself on your former neglect of my craft by chanting to you a trifle somewhat in unison with the thought you ask me to versify, but which you would not stay to hear at Tor Hadham (though you did drop a shilling into Max's tray)—it was one of the songs I sang that evening, and it was not ill received by my humble audience.

THE BEAUTY OF THE MISTRESS IS IN THE LOVER'S EYE.

"Is she not pretty, my Mabel May?
Nobody ever yet called her so.
Are not her lineaments faultless, say?
If I must answer you plainly—No.

"Joy to believe that the maid I love
None but myself as she is can see;
Joy that she steals from her Heaven above,
And is only revealed on this earth to me!"

As soon as he had finished this very artless ditty, the Minstrel rose and said:

"Now I must bid you good-bye. My way lies through those meadows, and yours, no doubt, along the high-road."

"Not so. Permit me to accompany you. I have a lodging not far from hence, to which the path through the fields is the shortest way."

The Minstrel turned a somewhat surprised and somewhat inquisitive look towards Kenelm. But feeling, perhaps, that having withheld from his fellow traveller all confidence as to his own name and attributes, he had no right to ask any confidence from that gentleman not voluntarily made to him, he courteously said "that he wished the way were longer, since it would be so pleasantly halved," and strode forth at a brisk pace.

The twilight was now closing into the brightness of a starry summer night, and the solitude of the fields was unbroken. Both these men, walking side by side, felt supremely happy. But happiness is like wine; its effect differing with the differing temperaments on which it acts. In this case garrulous and somewhat vaunting with the one man, warm-coloured, sensuous, impressionable to the influences of external nature, as an Æolian harp to the rise or fall of a passing wind; and, with the other man, taciturn and somewhat modestly expressed, saturnine, meditative, not indeed dull to the influences of external nature, but deeming them of no value, save where they passed out of the domain of the sensuous into that of the intellectual, and the soul of man dictated to the soul-less nature its own questions and its own replies.

The Minstrel took the talk on himself, and the talk charmed his listener. It became so really eloquent in the tones of its utterance, in the frank play of its delivery, that I could no more adequately describe it than a reporter, however faithful to every word a true orator may say, can describe that which, apart from all words, belongs to the presence of the orator himself.

Not, then, venturing to report the language of this singular itinerant, I content myself with saying that the substance of it was of the nature on which it is said most men can be eloquent:

it was personal to himself. He spoke of aspirations towards the achievement of a name, dating back to the dawn of memory; of early obstacles in lowly birth, stinted fortunes; of a sudden opening to his ambition, while yet in boyhood, through the generous favour of a rich man, who said, "The child has genius, I will give it the discipline of culture, one day it shall repay to the world what it owes to me;" of studies passionately begun, earnestly pursued, and mournfully suspended in early youth. He did not say how or wherefore: he rushed on to dwell upon the struggles for a livelihood for himself and those dependent on him; how in such struggles he was compelled to divert toil and energy from the systematic pursuit of the object he had once set before him; the necessities for money were too urgent to be postponed to the visions of fame. "But even," he exclaimed passionately, "even in such hasty and crude manifestations of what is within me, as circumstances limited my powers, I know that I ought to have found from those who profess to be authoritative judges the encouragement of praise. How much better, then, I should have done if I had found it! How a little praise warms out of a man the good that is in him, and the sneer of a contempt which he feels to be unjust chills the ardour to excel! However, I forced my way, so far as was then most essential to me, the sufficing bread-maker for those I loved; and in my holidays of song and ramble I found a delight that atoned for all the rest. But still the desire of fame, once conceived in childhood, once nourished through youth, never dies but in our grave. Foot and hoof may tread it down, bud, leaf, stalk; its root is too deep below the surface for them to reach, and year after year stalk and leaf and bud re-emerge. Love may depart from our mortal life; we console ourselves—the beloved will be reunited to us in the life to come. But if he who sets his heart on fame loses it in this life, what can console him?"

"Did you not say a little while ago that fame allowed of no grave?"

"True; but if we do not achieve it before we

ourselves are in the grave, what comfort can it give to us? Love ascends to heaven, to which we hope ourselves to ascend; but fame remains on the earth, which we shall never again revisit. And it is because fame is earth-born that the desire for it is the most lasting, the regret for the want of it the most bitter, to the child of earth. But I shall achieve it now; it is already in my grasp."

By this time the travellers had arrived at the brook, facing the wooden bridge beside Cromwell Lodge.

Here the Minstrel halted; and Kenelm, with a certain tremble in his voice, said, "Is it not time that we should make ourselves known to each other by name? I have no longer any cause to conceal mine, indeed I never had any cause stronger than whim—Kenelm Chillingly, the only son of Sir Peter, of Exmundham,——shire."

"I wish your father joy of so clever a son," said the Minstrel with his wonted urbanity. "You already know enough of me to be aware that I am of much humbler birth and station than you;

but if you chance to have visited the exhibition of the Royal Academy this year—ah! I understand that start—you might have recognized a picture of which you have seen the rudimentary sketch, 'The girl with the flower ball,' one of three pictures very severely handled by 'The Londoner,' but, in spite of that potent enemy, ensuring fortune and promising fame to the Wandering Minstrel whose name, if the sight of the pictures had induced you to inquire into that, you would have found to be Walter Melville. Next January I hope, thanks to that picture, to add 'Associate of the Royal Academy.' The public will not let them keep me out of it, in spite of 'The Londoner.' You are probably an expected guest at one of the more imposing villas from which we see the distant lights. I am going to a very humble cottage, in which henceforth I hope to find my established home. I am there now only for a few days, but pray let me welcome you there before I leave. The cottage is called Grasmere."

CHAPTER VI.

The Minstrel gave a cordial parting shake of the hand to the fellow-traveller whom he had advised to settle down, not noticing how very cold had become the hand in his own genial grasp. Lightly he passed over the wooden bridge, preceded by Max, and merrily, when he had gained the other side of the bridge, came upon Kenelm's ear, through the hush of the luminous night, the verse of the uncompleted love song:

> "Singing—singing,
> Lustily singing.
> Down the road with his dogs before,
> Came the Ritter of Nierestein."

Love song, uncompleted—why uncompleted? It was not given to Kenelm to divine the why. It was a love song versifying one of the prettiest fairy tales in the world, which was a great favourite with Lily, and which Lion had promised Lily to versify, but only to complete it in her presence, and to her perfect satisfaction.

CHAPTER VII.

If I could not venture to place upon paper the exact words of an eloquent coveter of fame, the earth-born, still less can I dare to place upon paper all that passed through the voiceless heart of a coveter of love, the heaven-born.

From the hour in which Kenelm Chillingly had parted from Walter Melville until somewhere between sunrise and noon the next day, the summer joyousness of that external nature which does now and then, though, for the most part, deceitfully, address to the soul of man questions and answers all her soul-less own, laughed away the gloom of his misgivings.

No doubt this Walter Melville was the beloved guardian of Lily; no doubt it was Lily whom he designated as reserved and reared to become his bride. But on that question Lily herself had the sovereign voice. It remained yet to be seen whether Kenelm had deceived himself in the belief that had made the world so beautiful to him since the hour of their last parting. At all events it was due to her, due even to his rival, to assert his own claim to her choice. And the more he recalled all that Lily had ever said to him of her guardian, so openly, so frankly, proclaiming affection, admiration, gratitude, the more convincingly his reasonings allayed his fears, whispering, "So might a child speak of a parent: not so does the maiden speak of the man she loves; she can scarcely trust herself to praise."

In fine, it was not in despondent mood, nor with dejected looks, that, a little before noon, Kenelm crossed the bridge and re-entered the enchanted land of Grasmere. In answer to his inquiries, the servant who opened the door said that neither Mr. Melville nor Miss Mordaunt were at home; they had but just gone out together for a walk. He was about to turn back, when Mrs. Cameron came into the hall, and, rather by gesture than words, invited him to enter. Kenelm followed her into the drawing-room, taking his seat beside her. He was about to speak, when she interrupted him in a tone of voice so unlike its usual languor, so keen, so sharp, that it sounded like a cry of distress.

"I was just about to come to you. Happily, however, you find me alone, and what may pass between us will be soon over. But first tell me—you have seen your parents; you have asked their consent to wed a girl such as I described; tell me, oh tell me that that consent is refused!"

"On the contrary, I am here with their full permission to ask the hand of your niece."

Mrs. Cameron sank back in her chair, rocking herself to and fro in the posture of a person in great pain.

"I feared that. Walter said he had met you last evening; that you, like himself, entertained the thought of marriage. You, of course, when you learnt his name, must have known with whom his thought was connected. Happily, he could not divine what was the choice to which your youthful fancy had been so blindly led."

"My dear Mrs. Cameron," said Kenelm very mildly, but very firmly, "you were aware of the purpose for which I left Moleswick a few days ago, and it seems to me that you might have forestalled my intention,· the intention which brings me thus early to your house. I come to say to Miss Mordaunt's guardian, 'I ask the hand of your ward. If you also woo her, I have a very noble rival. With both of us no consideration for our own happiness can be comparable to the duty of consulting hers. Let her choose between the two.'"

"Impossible!" exclaimed Mrs. Cameron; "impossible! You know not what you say; know not, guess not, how sacred are the claims of Walter Melville to all that the orphan whom he has protected from her very birth can give him in return. She has no right to a preference for another; her heart is too grateful to admit of one. If the choice were given to her between him and you, it is he whom she would choose. Solemnly I assure you of this. Do not, then, subject her to the pain of such a choice. Suppose, if you will, that you had attracted her fancy, and that now you proclaimed your love and urged your suit, she would not, must not, the less reject your hand, but you might cloud her happiness in accepting Melville's. Be generous. Conquer your own fancy; it can be but a passing one. Speak not to her, nor to Mr. Melville, of a wish which can never be realised. Go hence, silently, and at once."

The words and the manner of the pale imploring woman struck a vague awe into the heart of her listener. But he did not the less resolutely answer, "I cannot obey you. It seems to me that my honour commands me to prove to your niece that, if I mistook the nature of her feelings towards me, I did not, by word or look, lead her to believe mine towards herself were less in earnest than they are; and it seems scarcely less honourable towards my worthy rival to endanger his own future happiness, should he discover later that his bride would have been happier with another. Why be so mysteriously apprehensive? If, as you say, with such apparent conviction, there is no doubt of your niece's preference for another, at a word from her own lips I depart, and you will see me no more. But that word must be said by her; and if you will not permit me to ask for it in your own house, I will take my chance of finding her now, on her walk with Mr. Melville; and, could he deny me the right to speak to her alone, that which I would say can be said in his presence. Ah! madam, have you no mercy for the heart that you so needlessly torture? If I must bear the worst, let me learn it, and at once."

"Learn it, then, from my lips," said Mrs. Cameron, speaking with voice unnaturally calm, and features rigidly set into stern composure. "And I place the secret you wring from me under the seal of that honour, which you so vauntingly make your excuse for imperilling the peace of the home I ought never to have suffered you to enter. An honest couple, of humble station and narrow means, had an only son, who evinced in early childhood talents so remarkable that they attracted the notice of the father's employer, a rich man of very benevolent heart and very cultivated taste. He sent the child, at his expense, to a first-rate commercial school, meaning to provide for him later in his own firm. The rich man was the head partner of an eminent bank; but very infirm health, and tastes much estranged from business, had induced him to retire from all active share in the firm, the management of which was confined to a son whom he idolized. But the talents of the *protégé* he had sent to school, there took so passionate a direction towards art, and estranged from trade; and his designs in drawing when shown to connoisseurs, were deemed so promising of future excellence; that the patron changed his original intention, entered him as a pupil in the studio of a distinguished French painter, and afterwards bade him perfect his taste by the study of Italian and Flemish masterpieces.

"He was still abroad, when—" here Mrs. Cameron stopped, with visible effort, suppressed a sob, and went on, whisperingly, through teeth clenched together—"when a thunderbolt fell on the house of the patron, shattering his fortunes, blasting his name. The son, unknown to the father, had been decoyed into speculations, which proved unfortunate; the loss might have been easily retrieved in the first instance, unhappily he took the wrong course to retrieve it, and launched into new hazards. I must be brief. One day the world was startled by the news that a firm, famed for its supposed wealth and solidity, was bankrupt. Dishonesty, was alleged, was proved, not against the father,—he went forth from the trial, censured indeed for neglect, not condemned for fraud, but a penniless pauper. The—son—the son—the idolized son—was removed from the prisoner's dock, a convicted felon, sentenced to penal servitude. Escaped that sentence by—by—you guess—you guess. How could he escape except through death?—death by his own guilty deed."

Almost as much overpowered by emotion as Mrs. Cameron herself, Kenelm covered his bended face with one hand, stretching out the other blindly to clasp her own, but she would not take it.

A dreary foreboding. Again before his eyes rose the old grey tower—again in his ears thrilled the tragic tale of the Fletwodes. What was yet left untold held the young man in spell-bound silence. Mrs. Cameron resumed—

"I said the father was a penniless pauper; he died lingeringly bed-ridden. But one faithful friend did not desert that bed; the youth to whose genius his wealth had ministered. He had come from abroad with some modest savings from the sale of copies or sketches made in Florence. These savings kept a roof over the heads of the old man and the two helpless broken-hearted women—paupers like himself,—his own daughter and his son's widow. When the savings were gone, the young man stooped from his destined calling, found employment somehow, no matter how alien to his tastes, and these three whom his toil supported never wanted a home or food. Well, a few weeks after her husband's terrible death, his young widow (they had not been a year married) gave birth to a child—a girl. She did not survive the exhaustion of her con-

finement many days. The shock of her death
snapped the feeble thread of the poor father's life.
Both were borne to the grave on the same day.
Before they died, both made the same prayer to
their sole two mourners, the felon's sister, the old
man's young benefactor. The prayer was this,
that the new-born infant should be reared, however
humbly, in ignorance of her birth, of a
father's guilt and shame. She was not to pass a
suppliant for charity to rich and high-born kinsfolk,
who had vouchsafed no word even of pity
to the felon's guiltless father and as guiltless wife.
That promise has been kept till now. I am that
daughter. The name I bear, and the name which
I gave to my niece, are not ours, save as we may
indirectly claim them through alliances centuries
ago. I have never married. I was to have been
a bride, bringing to the representative of no
ignoble house what was to have been a princely
dower; the wedding day was fixed, when the
bolt fell. I have never again seen my betrothed.
He went abroad and died there. I think he
loved me, he knew I loved him. Who can blame

him for deserting me? Who could marry the felon's sister? Who would marry the felon's child? Who, but one? The man who knows her secret, and will guard it; the man who, caring little for other education, has helped to instil into her spotless childhood so steadfast a love of truth, so exquisite a pride of honour, that did she know such ignominy rested on her birth, she would pine herself away."

"Is there only one man on earth," cried Kenelm, suddenly, rearing his face,—till then concealed and downcast—and with a loftiness of pride on its aspect, new to its wonted mildness, "Is there only one man who would deem the virgin, at whose feet he desires to kneel and say, 'Deign to be the queen of my life,' not far too noble in herself to be debased by the sins of others before she was even born; is there only one man who does not think that the love of truth and the pride of honour are most royal attributes of woman or of man, no matter whether the fathers of the woman or the man were pirates as lawless as the fathers of Norman kings, or liars as unscrupulous, where their own interests were concerned, as have been the crowned representatives of lines as deservedly famous as Cæsars and Bourbons, Tudors and Stuarts? Nobility, like genius, is inborn. One man alone guard *her* secret!—guard a secret that if made known could trouble a heart that recoils from shame! Ah, madam, we Chillinglys are a very obscure undistinguished race, but for more than a thousand years we have been English gentlemen. Guard her secret rather than risk the chance of discovery that could give her a pang? I would pass my whole life by her side in Kamtchatka, and even there I would not snatch a glimpse of the secret itself with mine own eyes, it should be so closely muffled and wrapped round by the folds of reverence and worship."

This burst of passion seemed to Mrs. Cameron the senseless declamation of an inexperienced, hot-headed young man, and putting it aside, much as a great lawyer dismisses as balderdash the florid rhetoric of some junior counsel, rhetoric in which the great lawyer had once indulged, or as a woman for whom romance is over dismisses as idle verbiage some romantic sentiment that befools her young daughter, Mrs. Cameron simply replied, "All this is hollow talk, Mr. Chillingly; let us come to the point. After all I have said, do you mean to persist in your suit to my niece?"

"I persist."

"What!" she cried, this time indignantly, and with generous indignation; "What, even were it possible that you could win your parents' consent to marry the child of a man condemned to penal servitude, or, consistently with the duties a son owes to parents, conceal that fact from them, could you, born to a station on which every gossip will ask, 'Who and what is the name of the future Lady Chillingly?' believe that the who and the what will never be discovered! Have you, a mere stranger, unknown to us a few weeks ago, a right to say Walter Melville, 'Resign to me that which is your sole reward for the sublime sacrifices, for the loyal devotion, for the watchful tenderness of patient years!'"

"Surely, madam," cried Kenelm, more startled, more shaken in soul by this appeal, than by the previous revelations; "Surely, when we last parted, when I confided to you my love for your niece, when you consented to my proposal to return home, and obtain my father's approval of my suit; surely then was the time to say, 'No; a suitor with claims paramount and irresistible has come before you.'"

"I did not then know, Heaven is my witness, I did not then even suspect, that Walter Melville ever dreamed of seeking a wife in the child who had grown up under his eyes. You must own, indeed, how much I discouraged your suit; I could not discourage it more without revealing the secret of her birth, only to be revealed as an extreme necessity. But my persuasion was, that your father would not consent to your alliance with one so far beneath the expectations he was entitled to form, and the refusal of that consent would terminate all further acquaintance between you and Lily, leaving her secret undisclosed. It was not till you had left, only indeed two days ago, that I received from Walter Melville a letter, which told me what I had never before conjectured. Here is the letter, read it, and then say if you have the heart to force yourself into rivalry, with —with—" She broke off, choked by her exertion, thrust the letter into his hands, and with keen, eager, hungry stare watched his countenance while he read.

"——Street, Bloomsbury.

"My dear Friend,—Joy and triumph! My picture is completed; the picture on which, for so many months, I have worked night and day in this den of a studio, without a glimpse of the green fields, concealing my address from every one, even from you, lest I might be tempted to suspend my labours. The picture is completed—it is sold; guess the price? Fifteen hundred guineas, and to a dealer—a dealer! Think of that! It is to be carried about the country, exhibited by itself. You remember those three little landscapes of mine which two years ago I would gladly have sold for ten pounds, only neither

Lily nor you would let me. My good friend and earliest patron, the German merchant at Luscombe, who called on me yesterday, offered to cover them with guineas thrice piled over the canvas. Imagine how happy I felt when I forced him to accept them as a present. What a leap in a man's life it is when he can afford to say 'I give!' Now then, at last, at last I am in a position which justifies the utterance of the hope which has for eighteen years been my solace, my support; been the sunbeam that ever shone through the gloom, when my fate was at the darkest; been the melody that buoyed me aloft as in the song of the skylark, when in the voices of men I heard but the laugh of scorn. Do you remember the night on which Lily's mother besought us to bring up her child in ignorance of her parentage, not even communicate to unkind and disdainful relatives that such a child was born? do you remember how plaintively, and yet how proudly, she so nobly born, so luxuriously nurtured, clasping my hand when I ventured to remonstrate and say that her own family could not condemn her child because of the father's guilt,—she, the proudest woman I ever knew, she whose smile I can at rare moments detect in Lily, raised her head from her pillow, and gasped forth—

"'I am dying—the last words of the dying are commands. I command you to see that my child's lot is not that of a felon's daughter transported to the hearth of nobles. To be happy, her lot must be humble—no roof too humble to shelter, no husband too humble to wed, the felon's daughter.'

"From that hour I formed the resolve that I would keep hand and heart free, that when the grandchild of my princely benefactor grew up into womanhood I might say to her, 'I am humbly born, but thy mother would have given thee to me.' The new-born, consigned to our charge, has now ripened into woman, and I have now so assured my fortune that it is no longer poverty and struggle that I should ask her to share. I am conscious that, were her fate not so exceptional, this hope of mine would be a vain presumption—conscious that I am but the creature of her grandsire's bounty, and that from it springs all I ever can be—conscious of the disparity in years—conscious of many a past error and present fault. But, as fate so ordains, such considerations are trivial; I am her rightful choice. What other choice, compatible with these necessities which weigh, dear and honoured friend, immeasurably more on your sense of honour than they do upon mine, and yet mine is not dull? Granting, then, that you, her nearest and most responsible relative, do not contemn me for presumption, all else seems to me clear. Lily's child-like affection for me is too deep and too fond not to warm into a wife's love. Happily, too, she has not been reared in the stereotyped boarding-school shallownesses of knowledge and vulgarities of gentility; but educated, like myself, by the free influences of nature; longing for no halls and palaces save those that we build as we list, in fairyland; educated to comprehend and to share the fancies, which are more than book-lore to the worshipper of art and song. In a day or two, perhaps the day after you receive this, I shall be able to escape from London, and most likely shall come on foot as usual. How I long to see once more the woodbine on the hedge-rows, the green blades of the corn-field, the sunny lapse of the river, and dearer still the tiny falls of our own little noisy rill! Meanwhile I entreat you, dearest, gentlest, most honoured of such few friends as my life has hitherto won to itself, to consider well the direct purport of this letter. If you, born in a grade so much higher than mine, feel that it is unwarrantable insolence in me to aspire to the hand of my patron's grandchild, say so plainly; and I remain not less grateful for your friendship, than I was to your goodness when dining for the first time at your father's palace. Shy and sensitive and young, I felt that his grand guests wondered why I was invited to the same board as themselves. You, then courted, admired, you had sympathetic compassion on the raw, sullen boy; left those, who then seemed to me like the gods and goddesses of a heathen Pantheon, to come and sit beside your father's *protégé*, and cheeringly whisper to him such words as make a low-born, ambitious lad, go home light-hearted, saying to himself, 'Some day or other.' And what it is to an ambitious lad, fancying himself lifted by the gods and goddesses of a Pantheon, to go home light-hearted muttering to himself 'Some day or other,' I doubt if even you can divine.

"But should you be as kind to the presumptuous man as you were to the bashful boy, and say, 'Realized be the dream, fulfilled be the object of your life! take from me as her next of kin, the last descendant of your benefactor,' then I venture to address to you this request. You are in the place of mother to your sister's child, act for her as a keeper now, to prepare her mind and heart for the coming change in the relations between her and me. When I last saw her, six months ago, she was still so playfully infantine that it half seems to me I should be sinning against the reverence due to a child, if I said too abruptly, 'You are woman, and I love you not as child but as woman.' And yet, time is not allowed to me for long, cautious, and gradual slide from the relationship of friend into that of lover. I now understand what the great master of my art once said to me, 'A career is a destiny.' By one of those merchant princes who now at Manchester, as they did once at Genoa or Venice, reign alike over those two civilizers of the world which to dull eyes seem antagonistic, Art and Commerce, an offer is made to me for a picture on a subject which strikes his fancy; an offer so magnificently liberal that his commerce must command my art; and the nature of the subject compels me to seek the banks of the Rhine as soon as may be. I must have all the hues of the foliage in the meridian glories of summer. I can but stay at Grasmere a very few days; but before I leave I must know this, am I going to work for Lily or am I not? On the answer to that question depends all. If not to work for her, there would be no glory in the summer, no triumph in art to me: I refuse the offer. If she says 'Yes; it is for me you work,' then she becomes my destiny. She assures my career. Here I speak as an artist: nobody who is not an artist can guess how sovereign over even his moral being, at a certain critical epoch in his career of artist or his life of man, is the success or the failure of a single work. But I go on to speak as man. My love for Lily is such for the last six months, that though if she rejected me I should still serve art, still yearn for fame, it would be as an old man might do either. The youth of my life would be gone.

"As man I say, all my thoughts, all my dreams of happiness, distinct from Art and fame, are summed up in the one question—'Is Lily to be my wife or not?'

"Yours affectionately,

"W. M."

Kenelm returned the letter without a word.

Enraged by his silence, Mrs. Cameron exclaimed: "Now, sir, what say you. You have scarcely known Lily five weeks. What is the feverish fancy of five weeks' growth to the life-long devotion of a man like this! Do you now dare to say, 'I persist'?"

Kenelm waved his hand very quietly, as if to dismiss all conception of taunt and insult, and said with his soft melancholy eyes fixed upon the working features of Lily's aunt, "This man is more worthy of her than I. He prays you, in his letter, to prepare your niece for that change of relationship which he dreads too abruptly to break to her himself. Have you done so?"

"I have; the night I got the letter."

"And—you hesitate; speak truthfully, I implore. And—she—"

"She," answered Mrs. Cameron, feeling herself involuntarily compelled to obey the voice of that prayer, "She seemed stunned at first, muttering, 'This is a dream—it cannot be true—cannot! I Lion's wife—I—I! I, his destiny! In me his happiness!' And then she laughed her pretty child's laugh, and put her arms round my neck, and said, 'You are jesting, aunty. He could not write thus!' So I put that part of his letter under her eyes; and when she had convinced herself, her face became very grave, more like a woman's face than I ever saw it; and after a pause she cried out, passionately, 'Can you think me—can I think myself—so bad, so ungrateful, as to doubt what I should answer, if Lion asked me whether I would willingly say or do anything that made him unhappy? If there be such a doubt in my heart, I would tear it out by the roots, heart and all!' Oh! Mr. Chillingly. There would be no happiness for her with another, knowing that she had blighted the life of him to whom she owes so much, though she never will learn how much more she owes." Kenelm not replying to this remark, Mrs. Cameron resumed. "I will be perfectly frank with you, Mr. Chillingly. I was not quite satisfied with Lily's manner and looks the next morning, that is, yesterday. I did fear there might be some struggle in her mind in which there entered a thought of yourself. And when Walter, on his arrival here in the evening, spoke of you as one he had met before in his rural excursions, but whose name he only learned on parting at the bridge by Cromwell Lodge, I saw that Lily turned pale, and shortly afterwards went to her own room for the night. Fearing that any interview with you, though it would not alter her resolve, might lessen her happiness on the only choice she can and ought to adopt, I resolved to visit you this morning, and make that appeal to your reason and your heart which I have done now—not, I am sure, in vain. Hush! I hear his voice!"

Melville entered the room, Lily leaning on his arm. The artist's comely face was radiant with an ineffable joyousness. Leaving Lily, he reached Kenelm's side as with a single bound, shook him heartily by the hand, and saying—"I find that you have already been a welcomed visitor in this house. Long may you be so, so say I, so (I answer for her) says my fair betrothed, to whom I need not present you."

Lily advanced, and held out her hand very timidly. Kenelm touched rather than clasped it. His own strong hand trembled like a leaf.

He ventured but one glance at her face. All the bloom had died out of it, but the expression seemed to him wondrously, cruelly tranquil.

"Your betrothed—your future bride!" he said to the artist, with a mastery over his emotion rendered less difficult by the single glance at that tranquil face. "I wish you joy. All happiness to you, Miss Mordaunt. You have made a noble choice."

He looked round for his hat; it lay at his feet, but he did not see it; his eyes wandering away with uncertain vision, like those of a sleepwalker.

Mrs. Cameron picked up the hat and gave it to him.

"Thank you," he said meekly; then with a smile half sweet, half bitter, "I have so much to thank you for, Mrs. Cameron."

"But you are not going already—just as I enter too. Hold! Mrs. Cameron tells me you are lodging with my old friend Jones. Come and stop a couple of days with us, we can find you a room; the room over your butterfly cage, eh Fairy?"

"Thank you, too. Thank you all. No; I must be in London by the first train."

Speaking thus, he had found his way to the door, bowed with the quiet grace that characterized all his movements, and was gone.

"Pardon his abruptness, Lily; he too loves; he too is impatient to find a betrothed," said the artist gaily: "but now he knows my dearest secret, I think I have a right to know his; and I will try."

He had scarcely uttered the words before he too had quitted the room and overtaken Kenelm just at the threshold.

"If you are going back to Cromwell Lodge— to pack up, I suppose—let me walk with you as far as the bridge."

Kenelm inclined his head assentingly and tacitly as they passed through the garden-gate, winding backward through the lane which skirted the garden-pales; when, at the very spot in which the day after their first and only quarrel Lily's face had been seen brightening through the evergreen, that day on which the old woman, quitting her, said, "God bless you!" and on which the vicar, walking with Kenelm, spoke of her fairy charms; well, just in that spot Lily's face appeared again, not this time *brightening* through the evergreens, unless the palest gleam of the palest moon can be said to brighten. Kenelm saw, started, halted. His companion, then in the rush of a gladsome talk of which Kenelm had not heard a word, neither saw, nor halted; he walked on mechanically, gladsome and talking.

Lily stretched forth her hand through the evergreens. Kenelm took it reverentially. This time it was not his hand that trembled.

"Good-bye," she said in a whisper, "good-bye for ever in this world. You understand—you do understand me. Say that you do."

"I understand. Noble child—noble choice. God bless you. God comfort me!" murmured Kenelm. Their eyes met. Oh, the sadness; and, alas! oh the love in the eyes of both.

Kenelm passed on.

All said in an instant. How many Alls are said in an instant! Melville was in the midst of some glowing sentence, begun when Kenelm dropped from his side, and the end of the sentence was this:

"Words cannot say how fair seems life; how easy seems conquest of fame, dating from this day—this day"—and in his turn he halted, looked round on the sunlit landscape and breathed deep, as if to drink into his soul all of the earth's joy and beauty which his gaze could compass, and the arch of the horizon bound.

"They who knew her even the best," resumed the artist, striding on, "even her aunt never could guess how serious and earnest, under all her infantine prettiness of fancy, is that girl's real nature. We were walking along the brookside, when I began to tell how solitary the world would be to me if I could not win her to my side; while I spoke she had turned aside from the path we had taken, and it was not till we were under the shadow of the church in which we shall be married that she uttered the words that gives to every cloud in my fate the silver lining; implying thus how solemnly connected in her mind was the thought of love with the sanctity of religion."

Kenelm shuddered—the church—the burial-ground—the old gothic tomb—the flowers round the infant's grave!

"But I am talking a great deal too much about myself," resumed the artist. "Lovers are the most consummate of all egotists, and the most garrulous of all gossips. You have wished me joy on my destined nuptials, when shall I wish you joy on yours? Since we have begun to confide in each other, you are in my debt as to a confidence."

They had now gained the bridge. Kenelm turned round abruptly, "Good day; let us part here. I have nothing to confide to you that might not seem to your ears a mockery when I wish you joy." So saying, so obeying in spite of himself the anguish of his heart, Kenelm wrung his companion's hand with the force of an uncontrollable agony, and speeded over the bridge before Melville recovered his surprise.

The artist would have small claim to the essential attribute of genius, viz., the intuitive sympathy of passion with passion, if that secret of Kenelm's which he had so lightly said, "he had acquired the right to learn," was not revealed to him as by an electric flash. "Poor fellow!" he said to himself, pityingly; "how natural that he should fall in love with Fairy! but happily he is so young, and such a philosopher, that it is but one of those trials through which, at least ten times a year, I have gone with wounds that leave not a scar."

Thus soliloquising, the warm-blooded worshipper of Nature returned homeward, too blest in the triumph of his own love to feel more than a kindly compassion for the wounded heart, consigned with no doubt of the healing result to the fickleness of youth and the consolations of philosophy. Not for a moment did the happier rival suspect that Kenelm's love was returned; that an atom in the heart of the girl who had promised to be his bride, could take its light or shadow from any love but his own. Yet, more from delicacy of respect to the rival so suddenly self-betrayed, than from any more prudential motive, he did not speak even to Mrs. Cameron of Kenelm's secret and sorrow; and certainly neither she nor Lily was disposed to ask any question that concerned the departed visitor.

In fact the name of Kenelm Chillingly was scarcely, if at all, mentioned in that household during the few days which elapsed before Walter Melville quitted Grasmere for the banks of the Rhine, not to return till the autumn, when his marriage with Lily was to take place. During those days Lily was calm and seemingly cheerful —her manner towards her betrothed, if more subdued, not less affectionate than of old. Mrs. Cameron congratulated herself on having so successfully got rid of Kenelm Chillingly.

CHAPTER VIII.

So, then, but for that officious warning, uttered under the balcony at Luscombe, Kenelm Chillingly might never have had a rival in Walter Melville. But ill would any reader construe the character of Kenelm, did he think that such a thought increased the bitterness of his sorrow. No sorrow in the thought that a noble nature had been saved from the temptation to a great sin.

The good man does good merely by living. And the good he does may often mar the plans he formed for his own happiness. But he cannot regret that Heaven has permitted him to do good.

What Kenelm did feel is perhaps best explained in the letter to Sir Peter, which is here subjoined.

"MY DEAREST FATHER,—Never till my dying day shall I forget that tender desire for my happiness with which, overcoming all worldly considerations, no matter at what disappointment to your own cherished plans or ambition for the heir to your name and race, you sent me away from your roof, these words ringing in my ear like the sound of joy-bells, 'Choose as you will, with my blessing on your choice. I open my heart to admit another child—your wife shall be my daughter.' It is such an unspeakable comfort to me to recall those words now. Of all human affections gratitude is surely the holiest; and it blends itself with the sweetness of religion when it is gratitude to a father. And, therefore, do not grieve too much for me, when I tell you that the hopes which enchanted me when we parted are not to be fulfilled. Her hand is pledged to another—another with claims upon her preference to which mine cannot be compared; and he is himself, putting aside the accidents of birth and fortune, immeasurably my superior. In that thought—I mean the thought that the man she selects deserves her more than I do, and that in his happiness she will blend her own—I shall find comfort, so soon as I can fairly reason down the first all-engrossing selfishness that follows the sense of unexpected and irremediable loss. Meanwhile you will think it not unnatural that I resort to such aids for change of heart as are afforded by change of scene. I start for the Continent to-night, and shall not rest till I reach Venice which I have not yet seen. I feel irresistibly attracted towards still canals and gliding gondolas. I will write to you and to my dear mother the day I arrive. And I trust to write cheerfully, with full accounts of all I see and encounter. Do not, dearest father, in your letters to me revert or allude to that grief, which even the tenderest word from your own tender self might but chafe into pain more sensitive. After all, a disappointed love is a very common lot. And we meet every day men—ay, and women too—who have known it, and are thoroughly cured.

"The manliest of our modern lyrical poets has said very nobly and, no doubt, very justly,

'To bear is to conquer our fate.'

"Ever your loving son,

"K. C."

CHAPTER IX.

NEARLY a year and a half has elapsed since the date of my last chapter. Two Englishmen were —the one seated, the other reclined at length— on one of the mounds that furrow the ascent of Posilippo. Before them spread the noiseless sea, basking in the sunshine, without visible ripple; to the left there was a distant glimpse through gaps of brushwood of the public gardens and white water of the Chiaja. They were friends who had chanced to meet abroad—unexpectedly —joined company, and travelled together for many months, chiefly in the East. They had been but a few days in Naples. The elder of the two had important affairs in England which ought to have summoned him back long since. But he did not let his friend know this; his affairs seemed to him less important than the duties he owed to one for whom he entertained that deep and noble love which is something stronger than brotherly, for with brotherly affection it combines gratitude and reverence. He knew, too, that his friend was oppressed by a haunting sorrow, of which the cause was divined by one, not revealed by the other.

To leave him, so beloved, alone with that sorrow in strange lands, was a thought not to be cherished by a friend so tender; for in the friendship of this man there was that sort of tenderness which completes a nature, thoroughly manlike, by giving it a touch of the woman's.

It was a day which in our northern climates is that of winter; in the southern clime of Naples it was mild as an English summer day, lingering on the brink of autumn. The sun sloping towards the west, and already gathering around it roseate and purple fleeces. Elsewhere, the deep-blue sky was without a cloudlet.

Both had been for some minutes silent; at length the man reclined on the grass—it was the younger man—said suddenly, and with no previous hint of the subject introduced, "Lay your hand on your heart, Tom, and answer me truly. Are your thoughts as clear from regrets as the heavens above us are from a cloud? Man takes regret from tears that have ceased to flow, as the heaven takes cloud from the rains that have ceased to fall."

"Regrets? Ah, I understand, for the loss of the girl I once loved to distraction! No; surely I made that clear to you many, many, many months ago, when I was your guest at Moleswick."

"Ay, but I have never, since then, spoken to you on that subject. I did not dare. It seems to me so natural that a man, in the earlier struggle between love and reason, should say, 'reason shall conquer, and has conquered;' and yet—and yet—as time glides on, feel that the conquerors who cannot put down rebellion have a very uneasy reign. Answer me not as at Moleswick, during the first struggle, but now, in the after-day, when reaction from struggle comes."

"Upon my honour," answered the friend, "I

have had no reaction at all. I was cured entirely, when I had once seen Jessie again, another man's wife, mother to his child, happy in her marriage; and, whether she was changed or not—very different from the sort of wife I should like to marry, now that I am no longer a village farrier."

"And, I remember, you spoke of some other girl whom it would suit you to marry. You have been long abroad from her. Do you ever think of her—think of her still as your future wife? Can you love her? Can you, who have once loved so faithfully, love again?"

"I am sure of that. I love Emily better than I did when I left England. We correspond. She writes such nice letters." Tom hesitated, blushed, and continued timidly, "I should like to show you one of her letters."

"Do."

Tom drew forth the last of such letters from his breast pocket.

Kenelm raised himself from the grass, took the letter, and read slowly, carefully, while Tom watched in vain for some approving smile to brighten up the dark beauty of that melancholy face.

Certainly it was the letter a man in love might show with pride to a friend; the letter of a lady, well educated, well brought up, evincing affection modestly, intelligence modestly too; the sort of letter in which a mother who loved her daughter, and approved the daughter's choice, could not have suggested a correction.

As Kenelm gave back the letter, his eyes met his friend's. Those were eager eyes — eyes hungering for praise. Kenelm's heart smote him for that worst of sins in friendship — want of sympathy; and that uneasy heart forced to his lips congratulations, not perhaps quite sincere, but which amply satisfied the lover. In uttering them, Kenelm rose to his feet, threw his arm round his friend's shoulder, and said, "Are you not tired of this place, Tom? I am. Let us go back to England to-morrow." Tom's honest face brightened vividly. "How selfish and egotistical I have been!" continued Kenelm; "I ought to have thought more of you, your career, your marriage—pardon me——"

"Pardon you—pardon! Don't I owe to you all—owe to you Emily herself? If you had never come to Graveleigh, never said, 'Be my friend,' what should I have been now? what—what?"

The next day the two friends quitted Naples, *en route* for England, not exchanging many words by the way. The old loquacious crotchety humour of Kenelm had deserted him. A duller companion than he was you could not have conceived. He might have been the hero of a young lady's novel.

It was only when they parted in London that Kenelm evinced more secret purpose, more external emotion than one of his heraldic Daces shifting from the bed to the surface of a waveless pond.

"If I have rightly understood you, Tom, all this change in you, all this cure of torturing regret, was wrought—wrought lastingly—wrought so as to leave you heart-free for the world's actions and a home's peace, on that eve when you saw her whose face till then had haunted you, another man's happy wife, and in so seeing her, either her face was changed, or your heart became so."

"Quite true. I might express it otherwise but the fact remains the same."

"God bless you, Tom; bless you in your career without, in your home within," said Kenelm, wringing his friend's hand at the door of the carriage that was to whirl to love, and wealth, and station, the whilom bully of a village, along the iron groove of that contrivance, which, though now the tritest of prosaic realities, seemed once too poetical for a poet's wildest visions.

CHAPTER X.

A WINTER'S evening at Moleswick. Very different from a winter sunset at Naples. It is intensely cold. There has been a slight fall of snow, accompanied with severe, bright, clear frost, a thin sprinkling of white on the pavements. Kenelm Chillingly entered the town on foot, no longer a knapsack on his back. Passing through the main street, he paused a moment at the door of Will Somers. The shop was closed. No, he would not stay there to ask in a roundabout way for news. He would go in straightforwardly and manfully to Grasmere. He would take the inmates there by surprise. The sooner he could bring Tom's experience home to himself, the better. He had schooled his heart to rely on that experience, and it brought him back the old elasticity of his stride. In his lofty carriage and buoyant face were again visible the old haughtiness of the indifferentism that keeps itself aloof from the turbulent emotions and conventional frivolities of those whom its philosophy pities and scorns.

"Ha! ha!" laughed he who like Swift never laughed aloud, and often laughed inaudibly. "Ha! ha! I shall exorcise the ghost of my grief. I shall never be haunted again. If that stormy creature whom love might have maddened into crime, if *he* were cured of love at once by a single visit to the home of her whose face was changed to him—for the smiles and the tears of it had become the property of another man—how much more should I be left without a scar! I, the heir of the Chillinglys! I, the kinsman of a Mivers! I, the pupil of a Welby! I—I, Kenelm Chillingly, to be thus—thus—" Here, in the midst of his boastful soliloquy, the well-remembered brook rushed suddenly upon eye and ear, gleaming and moaning under the wintry moon. Kenelm Chillingly stopped, covered his face with his hands, and burst into a passion of tears.

Recovering himself slowly, he went on along the path, every step of which was haunted by the form of Lily.

He reached the garden gate of Grasmere, lifted the latch, and entered. As he did so, a man, touching his hat, rushed beside, and advanced before him—the village postman. Kenelm drew back, allowing the man to pass to the door, and as he thus drew back, he caught a side view of lighted windows looking on the lawn—the windows of the pleasant drawing-room in which he had first heard Lily speak of her guardian.

The postman left his letters, and regained the garden gate, while Kenelm still stood wistfully gazing on those lighted windows. He had, meanwhile, advanced along the whitened sward to the light, saying to himself, "Let me just see her and her happiness, and then I will knock boldly at the door, and say, 'Good evening, Mrs. Melville.'"

So Kenelm stole across the lawn, and stationing himself at the angle of the wall, looked into the window.

Melville, in dressing-robe and slippers, was seated alone by the fireside. His dog was lazily stretched on the hearth-rug. One by one the features of the room, as the scene of his vanished happiness, grew out from its stillness; the delicately-tinted walls; the dwarf bookcase, with its feminine ornaments on the upper shelf; the piano standing in the same place. Lily's own small low chair; *that* was not in its old place, but thrust into a remote angle as if it had passed into disuse. Melville was reading a letter, no doubt one of those which the postman had left. Surely the contents were pleasant, for his fair face, always frankly expressive of emotion, brightened wonderfully as he read on. Then he rose with a quick, brisk movement, and pulled the bell hastily.

A neat maid-servant entered — a strange face to Kenelm. Melville gave her some brief message. "He has had joyous news," thought Kenelm. "He has sent for his wife, that she may share his joy." Presently the door opened, and entered, not Lily, but Mrs. Cameron.

She looked changed. Her natural quietude of mien and movement the same, indeed, but with more languor in it. Her hair had become grey. Melville was standing by the table as she approached him. He put the letter into her hands with a gay, proud smile, and looked over her shoulder while she read it, pointing with his finger as to some lines that should more emphatically claim her attention.

When she had finished, her face reflected his smile. They exchanged a hearty shake of the hand, as if in congratulation. "Ah," thought Kenelm, "the letter is from Lily. She is abroad. Perhaps the birth of a first-born."

Just then Blanche, who had not been visible before, emerged from under the table, and as Melville re-seated himself by the fireside, sprang into his lap, rubbing herself against his breast. The expression of his face changed; he uttered some low exclamation. Mrs. Cameron took the creature from his lap, stroking it quietly, carried it across the room, and put it outside the door. Then she seated herself beside the artist, placing her hand in his, and they conversed in low tones, till Melville's face again grew bright, and again he took up the letter.

A few minutes later the maid-servant entered with the tea things, and after arranging them on the table approached the window. Kenelm retreated into the shade, the servant closed the shutters and drew the curtains — that scene of quiet home comfort vanished from the eyes of the looker on.

Kenelm felt strangely perplexed. What had become of Lily? was she indeed absent from her home? Had he conjectured rightly, that the letter which had evidently so gladdened Melville was from her, or was it possible—here a thought of joy seized his heart and held him breathless —was it possible that, after all, she had not married her guardian; had found a home elsewhere —was free? He moved on farther down the lawn, towards the water, that he might better bring before his sight that part of the irregular building in which Lily formerly had her sleeping-chamber, and her "own—own room." All was dark there; the shutters inexorably closed. The place with which the childlike girl had associated her most childlike fancies, taming and tending the honey drinkers destined to pass into fairies, that fragile tenement was not closed against the winds and snows; its doors were drearily open; gaps in the delicate wire-work; of its dainty draperies a few tattered shreds hanging here and there; and on the depopulated floor the moonbeams resting cold and ghostly. No spray from the tiny fountain; its basin chipped and mouldering; the scanty waters therein frozen. Of all the pretty wild ones that Lily fancied she could tame, not one. Ah! yes, there was one, probably not of the old familiar number; a stranger that might have crept in for shelter from the first blasts of winter, and now clung to an angle in the farther wall, its wings folded—asleep, not dead. But Kenelm saw it not; he noticed only the general desolation of the spot.

"Natural enough," thought he. "She has outgrown all such pretty silliness. A wife cannot remain a child. Still, if she had belonged to me...." The thought choked even his inward, unspoken utterance. He turned away, paused a moment under the leafless boughs of the great willow still dipping into the brook, and then with impatient steps strode back towards the garden gate.

"No—no—no. I cannot now enter that house and ask for Mrs. Melville. Trial enough for one night to stand on the old ground. I will return to the town. I will call at Jessie's, and there I can learn if she indeed be happy."

So he went on by the path along the brookside, the night momently colder and colder, and momently clearer and clearer, while the moon noiselessly glided into loftier heights. Wrapt in his abstracted thoughts, when he came to the spot in which the path split in twain he did not take that which led more directly to the town. His steps, naturally enough following the train of his thoughts, led him along the path with which the object of his thoughts was associated. He found himself on the burial ground, and in front of the old ruined tomb with the effaced inscription.

"Ah! child—child!" he murmured almost audibly, "what depths of woman tenderness lay concealed in thee! In what loving sympathy with the past—sympathy only vouchsafed to the tenderest women and the highest poets—didst thou lay thy flowers on the tomb, to which thou didst give a poet's history interpreted by a woman's heart, little dreaming that beneath the stone slept a hero of thine own fallen race."

He passed beneath the shadow of the yews, whose leaves no winter wind can strew, and paused at the ruined tomb—no flower now on its stone, only a sprinkling of snow at the foot of it—sprinklings of snow at the foot of each humbler grave mound. Motionless in the frosty air rested the pointed church spire, and through the frosty air, higher and higher up the arch of heaven, soared the unpausing moon. Around, and below, and above her, the stars which no science can number; yet not less difficult to number are the thoughts, desires, aspirations, which, in a space of time briefer than a winter's night, can pass through the infinite deeps of a human soul.

From his stand by the Gothic tomb, Kenelm looked along the churchyard for the infant's grave, which Lily's pious care had bordered with votive flowers. Yes, in that direction there was still a gleam of colour; could it be of flowers in that biting winter time—the moon is so deceptive, it silvers into the hue of the jessamines the green of the everlastings.

He passed towards the white grave mound. His sight had duped him; no pale flower, no green "everlasting" on its neglected border— only brown mould, withered stalks, streaks of snow.

"And yet," he said sadly, "she told me she had never broken a promise; and she had given a promise to the dying child. Ah! she is too happy now to think of the dead."

So murmuring, he was about to turn towards the town, when close by that child's grave he saw another. Round that other there were pale "everlastings," dwarfed blossoms of the laurestinus; at the four angles the drooping bud of a Christmas rose; at the head of the grave was a white stone, its sharp edges cutting into the star-lit air; and on the head, in fresh letters were inscribed these words:

To the Memory of
L. M.
Aged 17,
Died October 29, A.D. 18—.
This stone, above the grave to which her mortal remains are consigned, beside that of an infant not more sinless, is consecrated by those who most mourn and miss her.
ISABEL CAMERON,
WALTER MELVILLE.
"Suffer the little children to come unto me."

CHAPTER XI.

THE next morning Mr. Emlyn, passing from his garden to the town of Moleswick, descried a human form stretched on the burial ground, stirring restlessly but very slightly, as if with an involuntary shiver, and uttering broken sounds, very faintly heard, like the moans that a man in pain strives to suppress and cannot.

The rector hastened to the spot. The man was lying, his face downward, on a grave-mound, not dead, not asleep.

"Poor fellow! overtaken by drink, I fear," thought the gentle pastor; and as it was the habit of his mind to compassionate error even more than grief, he accosted the supposed sinner in very soothing tones—trying to raise him from the ground—and with very kindly words.

Then the man lifted his face from its pillow on the grave-mound, looked round him dreamily into the grey, blank air of the cheerless morn, and rose to his feet quietly and slowly.

The vicar was startled; he recognised the face of him he had last seen in the magnificent affluence of health and strength. But the character of the face was changed—so changed! its old serenity of expression, at once grave and sweet, succeeded by a wild trouble in the heavy eyelids and trembling lips.

"Mr. Chillingly—you! Is it possible?"

"Varus, Varus," exclaimed Kenelm passionately, "what hast thou done with my legions?"

At that quotation of the well-known greeting of Augustus to his unfortunate general, the scholar recoiled. Had his young friend's mind deserted him—dazed, perhaps, by over-study?

He was soon reassured; Kenelm's face settled back into calm, though a dreary calm, like that of the wintry day.

"I beg pardon, Mr. Emlyn; I had not quite shaken off the hold of a strange dream. I dreamed that I was worse off than Augustus; he did not lose the world when the legions he had trusted to another vanished into a grave."

Here Kenelm linked his arm in that of the rector—on which he leaned rather heavily—and drew him on from the burial ground into the open space where the two paths met.

"But how long have you returned to Moleswick?" asked Emlyn; "and how come you to choose so damp a bed for your morning slumbers?"

"The wintry cold crept into my veins when I stood in the burial ground, and I was very weary; I had no sleep at night. Do not let me take you out of your way; I am going on to Grasmere. So I see, by the record on a gravestone, that it is more than a year ago since Mr. Melville lost his wife."

"Wife? He never married."

"What!" cried Kenelm. "Whose, then, is that gravestone—'L. M.'?"

"Alas! it is our poor Lily's."

"And she died unmarried?"

As Kenelm said this he looked up, and the

sun broke out from the gloomy haze of the morning. "I may claim thee, then," he thought within himself—"claim thee as mine when we meet again."

"Unmarried—yes," resumed the vicar. "She was indeed betrothed to her guardian; they were to have been married in the autumn, on his return from the Rhine. He went there to paint on the spot itself his great picture, which is now so famous—'Roland, the Hermit Knight, looking towards the convent lattice for a sight of the Holy Nun.' Melville had scarcely gone before the symptoms of the disease which proved fatal to poor Lily betrayed themselves; they baffled all medical skill—rapid decline. She was always very delicate, but no one detected in her the seeds of consumption. Melville only returned a day or two before her death. Dear childlike Lily! how we all mourned for her!—not least the poor, who believed in her fairy charms."

"And least of all, it appears, the man she was to have married."

"He?—Melville? How can you wrong him so?

His grief was intense — overpowering — for the time."

"For the time! what time?" muttered Kenelm in tones too low for the pastor's ear.

They moved on silently. Mr. Emlyn resumed:

"You noticed the text on Lily's gravestone— 'Suffer the little children to come unto me'? She dictated it herself the day before she died. I was with her then, so I was at the last."

"Were you—were you—at the last—the last? Good day, Mr. Emlyn; we are just in sight of the garden gate. And—excuse me—I wish to see Mr. Melville alone."

"Well, then, good day; but if you are making any stay in the neighbourhood, will you not be our guest? We have a room at your service."

"I thank you gratefully; but I return to London in an hour or so. Hold, a moment. You were with her at the last? She was resigned to die?"

"Resigned! that is scarcely the word. The smile left upon her lips was not that of human resignation; it was the smile of a divine joy."

CHAPTER XII.

"Yes, sir, Mr. Melville is at home, in his studio."

Kenelm followed the maid across the hall into a room not built at the date of Kenelm's former visits to the house: the artist, making Grasmere his chief residence after Lily's death, had added it at the back of the neglected place wherein Lily had encaged "the souls of infants unbaptized."

A lofty room, with a casement partially darkened, to the bleak north; various sketches on the walls; gaunt specimens of antique furniture, and of gorgeous Italian silks, scattered about in confused disorder; one large picture on its easel curtained; another as large, and half finished, before which stood the painter. He turned quickly as Kenelm entered the room unannounced, let fall brush and pallet, came up to him eagerly, grasped his hand, drooped his head on Kenelm's shoulder, and said, in a voice struggling with evident and strong emotion:

"Since we parted, such grief! such a loss!"

"I know it; I have seen her grave. Let us not speak of it. Why so needlessly revive your sorrow? So—so—your sanguine hopes are fulfilled —the world at last has done you justice? Emlyn tells me that you have painted a very famous picture."

Kenelm had seated himself as he thus spoke. The painter still stood with dejected attitude on the middle of the floor, and brushed his hand over his moistened eyes once or twice before he answered, "Yes, wait a moment, don't talk of fame yet. Bear with me, the sudden sight of you unnerved me."

The artist here seated himself also on an old worm-eaten gothic chest, rumpling and chafing the golden or tinselled threads of the embroidered silk, so rare and so time-worn, flung over the gothic chest, so rare also, and so worm-eaten.

Kenelm looked through half-closed lids at the artist, and his lips, before slightly curved with a secret scorn, became gravely compressed. In Melville's struggle to conceal emotion the strong man recognised a strong man—recognised, and yet only wondered; wondered how such a man, to whom Lily had pledged her hand, could so soon after the loss of Lily go on painting pictures, and care for any praise bestowed on a yard of canvas.

In a very few minutes Melville recommenced conversation—no more reference to Lily than if she had never existed. "Yes, my last picture has been indeed a success, a reward complete, if tardy, for all the bitterness of former struggles made in vain, for the galling sense of injustice, the anguish of which only an artist knows, when unworthy rivals are ranked before him.

'Foes quick to blame, and friends afraid to praise.'

True, that I have still much to encounter, the cliques still seek to disparage me, but between me and the cliques there stands at last the giant form of the public, and at last critics of graver weight than the cliques have deigned to accord to me a higher rank than even the public yet acknowledge. Ah! Mr. Chillingly, you do not profess to be a judge of paintings, but, excuse me, just look at this letter. I received it only last night from the greatest connoisseur of my art, certainly in England, perhaps in Europe." Here Melville drew, from the side pocket of his picturesque *moyen âge* surtout, a letter signed by a name authoritative to all who—being painters themselves—acknowledge authority in one who could no more paint a picture himself than Addison, the ablest critic of the greatest poem modern Europe has produced, could have written ten lines of the Paradise Lost—and thrust the letter into Kenelm's hand. Kenelm read it listlessly, with an increased contempt for an artist who could so find in gratified vanity consolation for the life gone from earth. But, listlessly as he read the letter, the sincere and fervent enthusiasm of the laudatory contents impressed him, and the preeminent authority of the signature could not be denied.

The letter was written on the occasion of Melville's recent election to the dignity of R.A., successor to a very great artist whose death had created a vacancy in the Academy. He returned the letter to Melville, saying, "This is the letter I saw you reading last night as I looked in at your window. Indeed, for a man who cares for the opinion of other men, this letter is very flattering; and for the painter who cares for money, it must be very pleasant to know by how many guineas every inch of his canvas may be covered." Unable longer to control his passions of rage, of scorn, of agonizing grief, Kenelm then burst forth, "Man, Man, whom I once accepted as a teacher on human life, a teacher to warm, to brighten, to exalt mine own indifferent, dreamy, slow-pulsed self! has not the one woman whom thou didst select out of this over-crowded world to be bone of thy bone, flesh of thy flesh, vanished evermore from the earth—little more than a year since her voice was silenced, her heart ceased to beat? But how slight is such loss to thy life, compared to the worth of a compliment that flatters thy vanity!"

The artist rose to his feet with an indignant

impulse. But the angry flush faded from his cheek as he looked on the countenance of his rebuker. He walked up to him, and attempted to take his hand, but Kenelm snatched it scornfully from his grasp.

"Poor friend," said Melville, sadly and soothingly, "I did not think you loved her thus deeply. Pardon me." He drew a chair close to Kenelm's, and after a brief pause went on thus, in very earnest tones, "I am not so heartless, not so forgetful of my loss as you suppose. But reflect, you have but just learned of her death, you are under the first shock of grief. More than a year has been given to me for gradual submission to the decree of Heaven. Now listen to me, and try to listen calmly. I am many years older than you, I ought to know better the conditions on which man holds the tenure of life. Life is composite, many-sided, nature, does not permit it to be lastingly monopolized by a single passion, or, while yet in the prime of its strength, to be lastingly blighted by a single sorrow. Survey the great mass of our common race, engaged in the various callings, some the humblest, some the loftiest, by which the business of the world is carried on,—can you justly despise as heartless the poor trader, or the great statesman, when, it may be but a few days after the loss of some one nearest and dearest to his heart, the trader reopens his shop, the statesman reappears in his office? But in me, the votary of art, in me you behold but the weakness of gratified vanity—if I feel joy in the hope that my art may triumph, and my country may add my name to the list of those who contribute to her renown—where and whenever lived an artist not sustained by that hope, in privation, in sickness, in the sorrows he must share with his kind? Nor is this hope that of a feminine vanity, a sicklier craving for applause, it identifies itself with glorious services to our land, to our race, to the children of all after time. Our art cannot triumph, our name cannot live, unless we achieve a something that tends to beautify or ennoble the world in which we accept the common heritage of toil and of sorrow, in order, therefrom, to work out for successive multitudes a recreation and a joy."

While the artist thus spoke, Kenelm lifted towards his face eyes charged with suppressed tears. And the face, kindling as the artist vindicated himself from the young man's bitter charge, became touchingly sweet in its grave expression at the close of the not ignoble defence.

"Enough," said Kenelm rising. "There is a ring of truth in what you say. I can conceive the artist's, the poet's, escape from this world when all therein is death and winter, into the world he creates and colours at his will with the hues of summer. So, too, I can conceive how the man whose life is sternly fitted into the grooves of a trader's calling, or a statesman's duties, is borne on by the force of custom, afar from such brief halting spot as a grave. But I am no poet, no artist, no trader, no statesman; I have no calling, my life is fixed into no grooves. Adieu."

"Hold a moment. Not now, but somewhat

later, ask yourself whether any life can be permitted to wander in space, a monad detached from the lives of others. Into some groove or other, sooner or later, it must settle and be borne on obedient to the laws of nature and the responsibility to God."

CHAPTER XIII.

KENELM went back alone, and with downcast looks, through the desolate flowerless garden, when at the other side of the gate a light touch was laid on his arm. He looked up, and recognised Mrs. Cameron.

"I saw you," she said, "from my window coming to the house, and I have been waiting for you here. I wished to speak to you alone. Allow me to walk beside you."

Kenelm inclined his head assentingly, but made no answer.

They were nearly midway between the cottage and the burial-ground when Mrs. Cameron resumed, her tones quick and agitated contrasting her habitual languid quietude—

"I have a great weight on my mind; it ought not to be remorse. I acted as I thought in my conscience for the best. But oh, Mr. Chillingly, if I erred—if I judged wrongly, do say you at least forgive me." She seized his hand, pressing it convulsively. Kenelm muttered inaudibly—a sort of dreary stupor had succeeded to the intense excitement of grief. Mrs. Cameron went on—

"You could not have married Lily—you know you could not. The secret of her birth could not, in honour, have been concealed from your parents. They could not have consented to your marriage; and even if you had persisted, without that consent and in spite of that secret, to press for it—even had she been yours——"

"Might she not be living now?" cried Kenelm fiercely.

"No—no; the secret must have come out. The cruel world would have discovered it; it would have reached her ears. The shame of it would have killed her. How bitter then would have been her short interval of life! As it is, she passed away—resigned and happy. But I own that I did not, could not, understand her,

could not believe her feeling for you to be so
deep. I did think, that, when she knew her own
heart, she would find that love for her guardian
was its strongest affection. She assented, apparently without a pang, to become his wife; and
she seemed always so fond of him, and what girl
would not be? But I was mistaken—deceived.
From the day you saw her last, she began to fade
away; but then Walter left a few days after, and
I thought that it was his absence she mourned.
She never owned to me that it was yours—never
till too late—too late—just when my sad letter
had summoned him back only three days before
she died. Had I known earlier while yet there
was hope of recovery, I must have written to
you, even though the obstacles to your union
with her remained the same. Oh, again I implore you, say that if I erred you forgive me.
She did, kissing me so tenderly. She did forgive me. Will not you? It would have been
her wish."

"Her wish? Do you think I could disobey
it? I know not if I have anything to forgive.

If I have, how could I not forgive one who loved her? God comfort us both."

He bent down and kissed Mrs. Cameron's forehead. The poor woman threw her arm gratefully, lovingly round him, and burst into tears.

When she had recovered her emotion she said—

"And now, it is with so much lighter a heart that I can fulfil her commission to you. But, before I place this in your hands, can you make me one promise? Never tell Melville how she loved you. She was so careful he should never guess that. And if he knew it was the thought of union with him which had killed her, he would never smile again."

"You would not ask such a promise if you could guess how sacred from all the world I hold the secret that you confide to me. By that secret the grave is changed into an altar. Our bridals now are only awhile deferred."

Mrs. Cameron placed a letter in Kenelm's hand, and murmuring in accents broken by a sob, "She gave it to me the day before her last," left him, and with quick vacillating steps hurried back towards the cottage. She now understood *him*, at last, too well not to feel that on opening that letter he must be alone with the dead.

It is strange that we need have so little practical household knowledge of each other to be in love. Never till then had Kenelm's eyes rested upon Lily's handwriting. And he now gazed at the formal address on the envelope with a sort of awe. Unknown handwriting coming to him from an unknown world—delicate, tremulous handwriting—handwriting not of one grown up, yet not of a child who had long to live.

He turned the envelope over and over—not impatiently as does the lover whose heart beats at the sound of the approaching footstep, but lingeringly, timidly. He would not break the seal.

He was now so near the burial-ground. Where should the first letter ever received from her— the sole letter he ever could receive—be so reverentially, lovingly read, as at her grave?

He walked on to the burial-ground, sat down

by the grave, broke the envelope; a poor little ring, with a poor little single turquoise, rolled out and rested at his feet. The letter contained only these words:

"The ring comes back to you. I could not live to marry another. I never knew how I loved you—till, till I began to pray that you might not love me too much. Darling! darling! good-bye, darling!

"LILY.

"Don't let Lion ever see this, or ever know what it says to you. He is so good, and deserves to be so happy. Do you remember the day of the ring? Darling! darling!"

CHAPTER XIV.

SOMEWHAT more than another year has rolled away. It is early spring in London. The trees in the parks and squares are budding into leaf and blossom. Leopold Travers has had a brief but serious conversation with his daughter, and is now gone forth on horseback. Handsome and graceful still, Leopold Travers when in London is pleased to find himself scarcely less the fashion with the young than he was when himself in youth. He is now riding along the banks of the Serpentine, no one better mounted, better dressed, better looking, or talking with greater fluency on the topics which interest his companions.

Cecilia is in the smaller drawing-room, which is exclusively appropriated to her use—alone with Lady Glenalvon.

LADY GLENALVON: I own, my dear, dear Cecilia, that I range myself at last on the side of your father. How earnestly at one time I had hoped that Kenelm Chillingly might woo and win the bride that seemed to me most fitted to adorn and to cheer his life, I need not say. But when at Exmundham he asked me to befriend his choice of another, to reconcile his mother to that choice—evidently not a suitable one—I gave him up. And though that affair is at an end, he seems little likely ever to settle down to practical duties and domestic habits, an idle wanderer over the face of the earth, only heard of in remote places and with strange companions. Perhaps he may never return to England.

CECILIA: He is in England now, and in London.

LADY GLENALVON: You amaze me! Who told you so?

CECILIA: His father, who is with him. Sir Peter called yesterday, and spoke to me so kindly. Cecilia here turned aside her face to conceal the tears that had started to her eyes.

LADY GLENALVON: Did Mr. Travers see Sir Peter?

CECILIA: Yes; and I think it was something that passed between them which made my father speak to me—for the first time—almost sternly.

LADY GLENALVON: In urging Gordon Chillingly's suit.

CECILIA: Commanding me to reconsider my rejection of it. He has contrived to fascinate my father.

LADY GLENALVON: So he has me. Of course you might choose among other candidates for your hand one of much higher worldly rank, of much larger fortune, yet, as you have already rejected them, Gordon's merits became still more entitled to a fair hearing. He has already leapt into a position that mere rank and mere wealth cannot attain. Men of all parties speak highly of his parliamentary abilities. He is already marked in public opinion as a coming man—a future minister of the highest grade. He has youth and good looks, his moral character is without a blemish, yet his manners are so free from affected austerity, so frank, so genial. Any woman might be pleased with his companionship; and you with your intellect, your culture; you so born for high station; you of all women might be proud to partake the anxieties of his career, and the rewards of his ambition.

CECILIA (clasping her hands tightly together): I cannot, I cannot. He may be all you say—I know nothing against Mr. Chillingly Gordon—but my whole nature is antagonistic to his, and even were it not so——

She stopped abruptly, a deep blush warming up her fair face, and retreating to leave it coldly pale.

LADY GLENALVON (tenderly kissing her): You have not, then, even yet conquered the first maiden fancy; the ungrateful one is still remembered?

Cecilia bowed her head on her friend's breast, and murmured imploringly, "Don't speak against him, he has been so unhappy. How much he must have loved!"

"But it is not you whom he loved."

"Something here, something at my heart, tells me that he will love me yet; and if not, I am contented to be his friend."

CHAPTER XV.

WHILE the conversation just related took place between Cecilia and Lady Glenalvon, Gordon Chillingly was seated alone with Mivers in the comfortable apartment of the cynical old bachelor. Gordon had breakfasted with his kinsman, but that meal was long over; the two men having found much to talk about on matters very interesting to the younger, nor without interest to the elder one.

It is true that Chillingly Gordon had, within the very short space of time that had elapsed since his entrance into the House of Commons, achieved one of those reputations which mark out a man for early admission into the progressive career of office—not a very showy reputation, but a very solid one. He had none of the gifts of the genuine orator, no enthusiasm, no imagination, no imprudent bursts of fiery words from a passionate heart. But he had all the gifts of an exceedingly telling speaker — a clear, metallic voice; well-bred, appropriate action, not less dignified for being somewhat too quiet; readiness for extempore replies; industry and method for prepared expositions of principle or fact. But his principal merit with the chiefs of the assembly was in the strong good sense and worldly tact which made him a safe speaker. For this merit he was largely indebted to his frequent conferences with Chillingly Mivers. That gentleman, owing whether to his social qualities or to the influence of the 'Londoner' on public opinion, enjoyed an intimate acquaintance with the chiefs of all parties, and was up to his ears in the wisdom of the world. "Nothing," he would say, "hurts a young Parliamentary speaker like violence in opinion, one way or the other. Shun it. Always allow that much may be said on both sides. When the chiefs of your own side suddenly adopt a violence, you can go with them or against them according as best suits your own book."

"So," said Mivers, reclined on his sofa, and approaching the end of his second Trabuco (he never allowed himself more than two), "so I think we have pretty well settled the tone you must take in your speech to-night. It is a great occasion."

"True. It is the *first* time in which the debate has been arranged so that I may speak at ten o'clock or later. That in itself is a great leap; and it is a Cabinet Minister whom I am to answer—luckily, he is a very dull fellow. Do you think I might hazard a joke—at least a witticism?"

"At his expense? Decidedly not. Though his office compels him to introduce this measure, he was by no means in its favour when it was discussed in the Cabinet; and though, as you say, he is dull, it is precisely that sort of dulness which is essential to the formation of every respectable Cabinet. Joke at *him*, indeed! Learn that gentle dulness never loves a joke—at its own expense. Vain man! seize the occasion which your blame of his measure affords you to

secure his praise of yourself: compliment him.
Enough of politics. It never does to think too
much over what one has already decided to say.
Brooding over it, one may become too much in
earnest, and commit an indiscretion. So Kenelm
has come back?"

"Yes. I heard that news last night, at
White's, from Travers. Sir Peter had called on
Travers."

"Travers still favours your suit to the heiress?"

"More, I think, than ever. Success in Parliament has great effect on a man who has success in fashion and respects the opinion of clubs. But last night he was unusually cordial. Between you and me, I think he is a little afraid that Kenelm may yet be my rival. I gathered that from a hint he let fall of the unwelcome nature of Sir Peter's talk to him."

"Why has Travers conceived a dislike to poor Kenelm? He seemed partial enough to him once."

"Ay, but not as a son-in-law, even before I

had a chance of becoming so. And when, after Kenelm appeared at Exmundham while Travers was staying there, Travers learned, I suppose from Lady Chillingly, that Kenelm had fallen in love with and wanted to marry some other girl, who it seems rejected him, and still more when he heard that Kenelm had been subsequently travelling on the Continent in company with a low-lived fellow, the drunken, riotous son of a farrier, you may well conceive how so polished and sensible a man as Leopold Travers would dislike the idea of giving his daughter to one so little likely to make an agreeable son-in-law. Bah! I have no fear of Kenelm. By the way, did Sir Peter say if Kenelm had quite recovered his health? He was at death's door some eighteen months ago, when Sir Peter and Lady Chillingly were summoned to town by the doctors."

"My dear Gordon, I fear there is no chance of your succession to Exmundham. Sir Peter says that his wandering Hercules is as stalwart as ever, and more equable in temperament, more taciturn and grave—in short, less odd. But when you say you have no fear of Kenelm's rivalry, do you mean only as to Cecilia Travers?"

"Neither as to that nor as to anything in life; and as to the succession to Exmundham, it is his to leave as he pleases, and I have cause to think he would never leave it to me. More likely to Parson John or the parson's son—or why not to yourself? I often think that for the prizes immediately set before my ambition I am better off without land: land is a great obfuscator."

"Humph, there is some truth in that. Yet the fear of land and obfuscation does not seem to operate against your suit to Cecilia Travers?"

"Her father is likely enough to live till I may be contented to 'rest and be thankful' in the upper house; and I should not like to be a landless peer."

"You are right there; but I should tell you that, now Kenelm has come back, Sir Peter has set his heart on his son's being your rival."

"For Cecilia?"

"Perhaps; but certainly for Parliamentary reputation. The senior member for the county means to retire, and Sir Peter has been urged to allow his son to be brought forward—from what I hear, with the certainty of success."

"What! in spite of that wonderful speech of his on coming of age?"

"Pooh! that is now understood to have been but a bad joke on the new ideas, and their organs, including the 'Londoner.' But if Kenelm does come into the House, it will not be on your side of the question; and unless I greatly overrate his abilities—which very likely I do—he will not be a rival to despise. Except, indeed, that he may have one fault which in the present day would be enough to unfit him for public life."

"And what is that fault?"

"Treason to the blood of the Chillinglys. This is the age, in England, when one cannot be too much of a Chillingly. I fear that if Kenelm does become bewildered by a political abstraction —call it, no matter what, say, 'love of his country,' or some such old-fashioned crotchet—I fear—I greatly fear—that he may be—in earnest."

CHAPTER THE LAST.

It was a field night in the House of Commons—an adjourned debate, opened by George Belvoir, who had been, the last two years, very slowly creeping on in the favour, or rather the indulgence of the House, and more than justifying Kenelm's prediction of his career. Heir to a noble name and vast estates, extremely hard-working, very well informed, it was impossible that he should not creep on. That night he spoke sensibly enough, assisting his memory by frequent references to his notes; listened to courteously, and greeted with a faint "Hear hear!" of relief when he had done.

Then the House gradually thinned till nine o'clock, at which hour it became very rapidly crowded. A cabinet minister had solemnly risen, deposited on the table before him a formidable array of printed papers, including a corpulent blue book. Leaning his arm on the red box, he commenced with this awe-compelling sentence:

"Sir,—I join issue with the right honourable gentleman opposite. He says this is not raised as a party question. I deny it. Her Majesty's Government are put upon their trial."

Here there were cheers, so loudly, and so rarely greeting a speech from that cabinet minister, that he was put out, and had much to "hum" and to "ha," before he could recover the thread of his speech. Then he went on, with unbroken but lethargic fluency; read long extracts from the public papers, inflicted a whole page from the blue book, wound up with a peroration of respectable platitudes, glanced at the clock, saw that he had completed the hour which a cabinet minister who does not profess to be oratorical is expected to speak, but not to exceed; and sat down.

Uprose a crowd of eager faces, from which the Speaker, as previously arranged with the party whips, selected one—a young face, hardy, intelligent, emotionless.

I need not say that it was the face of Chillingly Gordon.

His position that night was one that required dexterous management and delicate tact. He habitually supported the Government; his speeches had been hitherto in their favour. On this occasion he differed from the Government. The difference was known to the chiefs of the opposition, and hence the arrangement of the whips, that he should speak for the first time after ten o'clock, and for the first time in reply to a cabinet minister. It is a position in which a young party man makes or mars his future. Chillingly Gordon spoke from the third row behind the Government; he had been duly cautioned by Mivers not to affect a conceited independence, or an adhesion to "violence" in ultra-liberal opinions, by seating himself below the gangway. Speaking thus, amid the rank and file of the Ministerial supporters, any opinion at variance with the mouth-pieces of the Treasury bench would be sure to produce a more effective sensation, than if delivered from the ranks of the mutinous Bashi

Bazouks divided by the gangway from better disciplined forces. His first brief sentences enthralled the House, conciliated the Ministerial side, kept the opposition side in suspense. The whole speech was, indeed, felicitously adroit, and especially in this, that while in opposition to the Government as a whole, it expressed the opinions of a powerful section of the cabinet, which, though at present a minority, yet being the most enamoured of a New Idea, the progress of the age would probably render a safe investment for the confidence which honest Gordon reposed in its chance of beating its colleagues.

It was not, however, till Gordon had concluded, that the cheers of his audience—impulsive and hearty as are the cheers of that assembly, when the evidence of intellect is unmistakable—made manifest to the Gallery and the reporters the full effect of the speech he had delivered. The chief of the opposition whispered to his next neighbour, "I wish we could get that man." The cabinet minister whom Gordon had answered—more pleased with a personal compliment to himself than displeased with an attack on the measure his office compelled him to advocate—whispered to his chief, "That is a man we must not lose."

Two gentlemen in the Speaker's gallery, who had sat there from the opening of the debate, now quitted their places. Coming into the lobby, they found themselves commingled with a crowd of members who had also quitted their seats, after Gordon's speech, in order to discuss its merits, as they gathered round the refreshment table for oranges or soda-water. Among them was George Belvoir, who on sight of the younger of the two gentlemen issuing from the Speaker's Gallery, accosted him with friendly greeting:

"Ha! Chillingly, how are you? Did not know you were in town. Been here all the evening? Yes; very good debate. How did you like Gordon's speech?"

"I liked yours much better."

"Mine!" cried George, very much flattered and very much surprised. "Oh! mine was a mere humdrum affair, a plain statement of the reasons for the vote I should give. And Gordon's was anything but that. You did not like his opinions?"

"I don't know what his opinions are. But I did not like his ideas."

"I don't quite understand you. What ideas?"

"The new ones; by which it is shown how rapidly a great State can be made small."

Here Mr. Belvoir was taken aside by a brother member, on an important matter to be brought before the committee on salmon fisheries, on which they both served; and Kenelm, with his companion, Sir Peter, threaded his way through the crowded lobby, and disappeared. Emerging into the broad space, with its lofty clock tower, Sir Peter halted, and pointing towards the old Abbey, half in shadow, half in light, under the tranquil moonbeams, said:

"It tells much for the duration of a people, when it accords with the instinct of immortality in a man; when an honoured tomb is deemed recompense for the toils and dangers of a noble life. How much of the history of England Nelson summed up in the simple words: 'Victory or Westminster Abbey.'"

"Admirably expressed, my dear father," said Kenelm briefly.

"I agree with your remark, which I overheard, on Gordon's speech," resumed Sir Peter. "It was wonderfully clever; yet I should have been sorry to hear you speak it. It is not by such sentiments that Nelsons become great. If such sentiments should ever be national, the cry will not be 'Victory or Westminster Abbey!' but 'Defeat and the Three per Cents!'"

Pleased with his own unwonted animation, and with the sympathizing half-smile on his son's taciturn lips, Sir Peter then proceeded more immediately to the subjects which pressed upon his heart. Gordon's success in Parliament, Gordon's suit to Cecilia Travers, favoured, as Sir Peter had learned, by her father, rejected as yet by herself, were somehow inseparably mixed up in Sir Peter's mind and his words, as he sought to kindle his son's emulation. He dwelt on the obligations which a country imposed on its citizens, especially on the young and vigorous generation to which the destinies of those to follow were entrusted; and with these stern obligations he combined all the cheering and tender associations which an English public man connects with an English home: the wife with a smile to soothe the cares, and a mind to share the aspirations, of a life that must go through labour to achieve renown; thus, in all he said, binding together, as if they could not be disparted, Ambition and Cecilia.

His son did not interrupt him by a word: Sir Peter in his eagerness not noticing that Kenelm had drawn him aside from the direct thoroughfare, and had now made halt in the middle of Westminster Bridge, bending over the massive parapet and gazing abstractedly upon the waves of the starlit river. On the right the stately length of the people's legislative palace, so new in its date, so elaborately in each detail ancient in its form, stretching on towards the lowly and jagged roofs of penury and crime. Well might these be so near to the halls of a people's legislative palace;—near to the heart of every legislator for a people must be the mighty problem how to increase a people's splendour and its virtue, and how to diminish its penury and its crime.

"How strange it is," said Kenelm, still bending over the parapet, "that throughout all my desultory wanderings I have ever been attracted towards the sight and the sound of running waters, even those of the humblest rill! Of what thoughts, of what dreams, of what memories, colouring the history of my past, the waves of the humblest rill could speak, were the waves themselves not such supreme philosophers — roused indeed on their surface, vexed by a check to their own course, but so indifferent to all that makes gloom or death to the mortals who think and dream and feel beside their banks."

"Bless me," said Sir Peter to himself, "the boy has got back to his old vein of humours and melancholies. He has not heard a word I have been saying. Travers is right. He will never do anything in life. Why did I christen him Kenelm? he might as well have been christened Peter."

Still, loth to own that his eloquence had been expended in vain, and that the wish of his heart was doomed to expire disappointed, Sir Peter said aloud, "You have not listened to what I said; Kenelm, you grieve me."

"Grieve you! you! do not say that, father, dear father. Listen to you! Every word you have said has sunk into the deepest deep of my heart. Pardon my foolish purposeless snatch of talk to myself, it is but my way, only my way, dear father!"

"Boy, boy," cried Sir Peter, with tears in his voice, "if you could get out of those odd ways of yours I should be so thankful. But if you cannot, nothing you can do shall grieve me. Only, let me say this; running waters have had a great charm for you. With a humble rill you associate thoughts, dreams, memories in your past. But now you halt by the stream of the mighty river—before you the senate of an empire wider than Alexander's; behind you the market of a commerce to which that of Tyre was a pitiful trade. Look farther down, those squalid hovels, how much there to redeem or to remedy; and out of sight, but not very distant, the nation's Walhalla: 'Victory or Westminster Abbey!' The humble rill has witnessed your past. Has the mighty river no effect on your future? The rill keeps no record of your past, shall the river keep no record of your future? Ah, boy, boy, I see you are dreaming still—no use talking. Let us go home."

"I was not dreaming, I was telling myself that the time had come to replace the old Kenelm with the new ideas, by a New Kenelm with the Ideas of Old. Ah! perhaps we must—at whatever cost to ourselves,—we must go through the romance of life before we clearly detect what is grand in its realities. I can no longer lament that I stand estranged from the objects and pursuits of my race. I have learned how much I have with them in common. I have known love; I have known sorrow."

Kenelm paused a moment, only a moment, then lifted the head which, during that pause, had drooped, and stood erect at the full height of his stature; startling his father by the change that had passed over his face; lip — eye — his whole aspect eloquent with a resolute enthusiasm, too grave to be the flash of a passing moment.

"Ay, ay," he said, "Victory or Westminster Abbey! The world is a battle-field in which the worst wounded are the deserters, stricken as they seek to fly, and hushing the groans that would betray the secret of their inglorious hiding-place. The pain of wounds received in the thick of the fight, is scarcely felt in the joy of service to some honoured cause, and is amply atoned by the reverence for noble scars. My choice is made. Not that of deserter, that of soldier in the ranks."

"It will not be long before you rise from the ranks, my boy, if you hold fast to the Idea of Old, symbolised in the English battle-cry: 'Victory or Westminster Abbey.'"

So saying, Sir Peter took his son's arm, leaning on it proudly; and so, into the crowded thoroughfares, from the halting place on the modern bridge that spans the legendary river, passes the Man of the Young Generation to fates beyond the verge of the horizon to which the eyes of *my* generation must limit their wistful gaze.

THE END.

PRINTING OFFICE OF THE PUBLISHER.

March  1873.

Tauchnitz Edition.

Each volume 1½ Thaler = 2 Francs.

CONTENTS:

Latest Volumes . . . . . . Page 2.
Collection of British Authors,
    vol. 1—1303 . . . . . . „ 3-13.
Series for the Young, vol. 1—20 „ 14.
Collection of German Authors,
    vol. 1—21 . . . . „ 15.
Dictionaries . . . . „ 16.

Sold by all the principal booksellers on the Continent.

March 1873.

Tauchnitz Edition, Latest Volumes.

Off the Skelligs by Jean Ingelow, 3 vols.
Historical Essays by Edward A. Freeman, 1 vol.
A Mingled Yarn by the Author of 'Sunbeam Stories,' 2 v.
The Yellow Flag by Edmund Yates, 2 vols.
Joan Merryweather by Katherine Saunders, 1 vol.
Friends in Council by Sir Arthur Helps, 2 vols.

Collection of British Authors.

Rev. W. Adams:
Sacred Allegories 1 v.

Miss Aguilar:
Home Influence 2 v. The Mother's Recompense 2 v.

Hamilton Aïdé:
Rita 1 v. Carr of Carrlyon 2 v. The Marstons 2 v. In that State of Life 1 v. Morals and Mysteries 1 v.

W. Harrison Ainsworth:
Windsor Castle 1 v. Saint James's 1 v. Jack Sheppard (w. portrait) 1 v. The Lancashire Witches 2 v. The Star-Chamber 2 v. The Flitch of Bacon 1 v. The Spendthrift 1 v. Mervyn Clitheroe 2 v. Ovingdean Grange 1 v. The Constable of the Tower 1 v. The Lord Mayor of London 2 v. Cardinal Pole 2 v. John Law 2 v. The Spanish Match 2 v. The Constable de Bourbon 2 v. Old Court 2 v. Myddleton Pomfret 2 v. The South-Sea Bubble 2 v. Hilary St. Ives 2 v. Talbot Harland 1 v. Tower Hill 1 v. Boscobel; or, the Royal Oak 2 v.

"All for Greed,"
Author of—
All for Greed 1 v. Love the Avenger 2 v.

Miss Austen:
Sense and Sensibility 1 v. Mansfield Park 1 v. Pride and Prejudice 1 v. Northanger Abbey, and Persuasion 1 v.

Nina Balatka 1 v.

Rev. R. H. Baynes:
Lyra Anglicana, Hymns and Sacred Songs 1 v.

Currer Bell
(Charlotte Brontë):
Jane Eyre 2 v. Shirley 2 v. Villette 2 v. The Professor 1 v.

Ellis & Acton Bell:
Wuthering Heights, and Agnes Grey 2 v.

Isa Blagden:
The Woman I loved, and the Woman who loved me; A Tuscan Wedding 1 v.

William Black:
A Daughter of Heth 2 v. In Silk Attire 2 v. The strange Adventures of a Phaeton 2 v.

Lady Blessington:
Meredith 1 v. Strathern 2 v. Memoirs of a Femme de Chambre 1 v. Marmaduke Herbert 2 v. Country Quarters (w. portrait) 2 v.

Miss Braddon:
Lady Audley's Secret 2 v. Aurora Floyd 2 v. Eleanor's Vic-

The price of each volume is ½ Thaler = 2 Francs.

tory 2 v. John Marchmont's Legacy 2 v. Henry Dunbar 2 v. The Doctor's Wife 2 v. Only a Clod 2 v. Sir Jasper's Tenant 2 v. The Lady's Mile 2 v. Rupert Godwin 2 v. Dead-Sea Fruit 2 v. Run to Earth 2 v. Fenton's Quest 2 v. The Lovels of Arden 2 v.

Shirley Brooks:
The Silver Cord 3 v. Sooner or Later 3 v.

Miss Rhoda Broughton:
Cometh up as a Flower 1 v. Not wisely, but too well 2 v. Red as a Rose is She 2 v. Tales for Christmas Eve 1 v.

John Brown:
Rab and his Friends, and other Tales 1 v.

Eliz. Barrett Browning:
A Selection from her Poetry (w. portrait) 1 v. Aurora Leigh 1 v.

Robert Browning:
Poetical Works (w. portrait) 2 v.

Bulwer (Lord Lytton):
Pelham (w. portrait) 1 v. Eugene Aram 1 v. Paul Clifford 1 v. Zanoni 1 v. The Last Days of Pompeii 1 v. The Disowned 1 v. Ernest Maltravers 1 v. Alice 1 v. Eva, and the Pilgrims of the Rhine 1 vol. Devereux 1 v. Godolphin, and Falkland 1 v. Rienzi 1 v. Night and Morning 1 v. The Last of the Barons 2 v. Athens 2 v. The Poems and Ballads of Schiller 1 v. Lucretia 2 v. Harold 2 v. King Arthur 2 v. The new Timon; St Stephen's 1 v. The Caxtons 2 v. My Novel 4 v. What will he do with it? 4 v. The Dramatic Works 2 v. A Strange Story 2 v. Caxtoniana 2 v. The Lost Tales of Miletus 1 v. Miscellaneous Prose Works 4 v. The Odes and Epodes of Horace 2 v.

Henry Lytton Bulwer (Lord Dalling):
Historical Characters 2 v. The Life of Henry John Temple, Viscount Palmerston 2 v.

John Bunyan:
The Pilgrim's Progress 1 v.

Buried Alone 1 v.

Miss Burney:
Evelina 1 v.

Robert Burns:
Poetical Works (w. portrait) 1 v.

Lord Byron:
Poetical Works (w. portrait) 5 v.

Thomas Carlyle:
The French Revolution 3 v. Frederick the Great 13 v. Oliver Cromwell's Letters and Speeches 4 v. The Life of Friedrich Schiller 1 v.

The price of each volume is ½ Thaler = 2 Francs.

Collection of British Authors Tauchnitz Edition.

"Chronicles of the Schönberg-Cotta Family," Author of—
Chronicles of the Schönberg-Cotta Family 2 v. The Draytons and the Davenants 2 v. On Both Sides of the Sea 2 v. Winifred Bertram 1 v. Diary of Mrs. Kitty Trevylyan 1 v. The Victory of the Vanquished 1 v. The Cottage by the Cathedral 1 v.

Coleridge:
The Poems 1 v.

Wilkie Collins:
After Dark 1 v. Hide and Seek 2 v. A Plot in Private Life 1 v. The Woman in White 2 v, Basil 1 v. No Name 3 v. The Dead Secret 2 v. Antonina 2 v. Armadale 3 v. The Moonstone 2 v. Man and Wife 3 v, Poor Miss Finch 2 v. Miss or Mrs.? 1 v.

Fenimore Cooper:
The Spy (w. portrait) 1 v. The two Admirals 1 v. The Jack O'Lantern 1 v.

Mrs. Craik (Miss Mulock):
John Halifax, Gentleman 2 v. The Head of the Family 2 v. A Life for a Life 2 v. A Woman's Thoughts about Women 1 v. Agatha's Husband 1 v. Romantic Tales 1 v. Domestic Stories 1 v. Mistress and Maid 1 v. The Ogilvies 1 v. Lord Erlistoun 1 v. Christian's Mistake 1 v. Bread upon the Waters 1 v. A Noble Life 1 v. Olive 2 v. Two Marriages 1 v. Studies from Life 1 v. Poems 1 v. The Woman's Kingdom 2 v. The Unkind Word 2 v. A Brave Lady 2 v. Hannah 2 v. Fair France 1 v.

Miss Georgiana Craik:
Lost and Won 1 v. Faith Unwin's Ordeal 1 v. Leslie Tyrrell 1 v. Winifred's Wooing, and other Tales 1 v. Mildred 1 v. Esther Hill's Secret 2 v. Hero Trevelyan 1 v. Without Kith or Kin 2 v.

Miss Cummins:
The Lamplighter 1 v. Mabel Vaughan 1 v. El Fureidîs 1 v. Haunted Hearts 1 v.

De-Foe:
The Life and surprising Adventures of Robinson Crusoe 1 v.

Charles Dickens:
The Posthumous Papers of the Pickwick Club (w. portrait) 2 v. American Notes 1 v. Oliver Twist 1 v. The Life and Adventures of Nicholas Nickleby 2 v. Sketches 1 v. The Life and Adventures of Martin Chuzzlewit 2 v. A Christmas Carol; the Chimes; the Cricket on the Hearth 1 v. Master Humphrey's Clock (Old Curiosity Shop, Barnaby Rudge, and other Tales) 3 v. Pictures from Italy 1 v. The Battle of Life; the Haunted Man 1 v. Dombey and Son 3 v. David Copperfield 3 v. Bleak House 4 v. A Child's History of England (2 v. 8° 27 Ngr.) Hard Times 1 v. Little Dorrit 4 v. A Tale

The price of each volume is ½ Thaler = 2 Francs.

of two Cities 2 v. Hunted Down; The Uncommercial Traveller 1 v. Great Expectations 2 v. Christmas Stories 1 v. Our Mutual Friend 4 v. Somebody's Luggage; Mrs. Lirriper's Lodgings; Mrs. Lirriper's Legacy 1 v. Doctor Marigold's Prescriptions; Mugby Junction 1 v. No Thoroughfare 1 v. The Mystery of Edwin Drood 2 v.

B. Disraeli:
Coningsby 1 v. Sybil 1 v. Contarini Fleming (w. portrait) 1 v. Alroy 1 v. Tancred 2 v. Venetia 2 v. Vivian Grey 2 v. Henrietta Temple 1 v. Lothair 2 v.

W. Hepworth Dixon:
Personal History of Lord Bacon 1 v. The Holy Land 2 v. New America 2 v. Spiritual Wives 2 v. Her Majesty's Tower 4 v. Free Russia 2 v.

Miss Amelia B. Edwards:
Barbara's History 2 v. Miss Carew 2 v. Hand and Glove 1 v. Half a Million of Money 2 v. Debenham's Vow 2 v. In the Days of my Youth 2 v.

Miss M. Betham Edwards:
The Sylvestres 1 v.

Mrs. Edwardes:
Archie Lovell 2 v. Steven Lawrence, Yeoman 2 v. Ought we to Visit her? 2 v.

Mrs. Elliot:
Diary of an Idle Woman in Italy 2 v.

George Eliot:
Scenes of Clerical Life 2 v. Adam Bede 2 v. The Mill on the Floss 2 v. Silas Marner 1 v. Romola 2 v. Felix Holt 2 v.

Essays and Reviews 1 v.

Estelle Russell 2 v.

Expiated 2 v.

Fielding:
The History of Tom Jones 2 v.

Five Centuries
of the English Language and Literature 1 v.

A. Forbes:
My Experiences of the War between France and Germany 2 v. Soldiering and Scribbling 1 v.

John Forster:
The Life of Charles Dickens v. 1-4.

"Found Dead," Author of—
Found Dead 1 v. Gwendoline's Harvest 1 v. Like Father, like Son 2 v. Not Wooed, but Won 2 v. Cecil's Tryst 1 v. A Woman's Vengeance 2 v.

Frank Fairlegh 2 v.

Edward A. Freeman:
The Growth of the English Constitution 1 v. Select Historical Essays 1 v.

Lady G. Fullerton:
Ellen Middleton 1 v. Grantley Manor 2 v. Lady Bird 2 v. Too Strange not to be True 2 v. Constance Sherwood 2 v. A stormy Life 2 v. Mrs. Gerald's Niece 2 v.

The price of each volume is ½ Thaler = 2 Francs.

Mrs. Gaskell:
Mary Barton 1 v. Ruth 2 v. North and South 1 v. Lizzie Leigh 1 v. The Life of Charlotte Brontë 2 v. Lois the Witch 1 v. Sylvia's Lovers 2 v. A Dark Night's Work 1 v. Wives and Daughters 3 v. Cranford 1 v. Cousin Phillis, and other Tales 1 v.

Goldsmith:
Select Works: The Vicar of Wakefield; Poems; Dramas (w. portrait) 1 v.

Mrs. Gore:
Castles in the Air 1 v. The Dean's Daughter 2 v. Progress and Prejudice 2 v. Mammon 2 v. A Life's Lessons 2 v. The two Aristocracies 2 v. Heckington 2 v.

"Guy Livingstone,"
Author of—
Guy Livingstone 1 v. Sword and Gown 1 v. Barren Honour 1 v. Border and Bastille 1 v. Maurice Dering 1 v. Sans Merci 2 v. Breaking a Butterfly 2 v. Anteros 2 v.

Mrs. S. C. Hall:
Can Wrong be Right? 1 v.

Bret Harte:
Prose and Poetry 2 v.

Sir H. Havelock,
by the Rev. W. Brock, 1 v.

Nathaniel Hawthorne:
The Scarlet Letter 1 v. Transformation 2 v. Passages from the English Note-Books 2 v.

Sir Arthur Helps:
Friends in Council 2 v.

Mrs. Hemans:
The Select Poetical Works 1 v.

Mrs. Cashel Hoey:
A Golden Sorrow 2 v.

Household Words
conducted by Ch. Dickens. 1851-56. 36 v. NOVELS and TALES reprinted from Households Words by Ch. Dickens. 1856-59. 11 v.

Thos. Hughes:
Tom Brown's School Days 1 v.

Jean Ingelow:
Off the Skelligs 3 v.

Washington Irving:
The Sketch Book (w. portrait) 1 v. The Life of Mahomet 1 v. Successors of Mahomet 1 v. Oliver Goldsmith 1 v. Chronicles of Wolfert's Roost 1 v. Life of George Washington 5 v.

G. P. R. James:
Morley Ernstein (w. portrait) 1 v. Forest Days 1 v. The False Heir 1 v. Arabella Stuart 1 v. Rose d'Albret 1 v. Arrah Neil 1 v. Agincourt 1 v. The Smuggler 1 v. The Step-Mother 2 v. Beauchamp 1 v. Heidelberg 1 v. The Gipsy 1 v. The Castle of Ehrenstein 1 v. Darnley 1 v. Russell 2 v. The Convict 2 v. Sir Theodore Broughton 2 v.

J. Cordy Jeaffreson:
A Book about Doctors 2 v. A Woman in Spite of herself 2 v.

The price of each volume is ½ Thaler = 2 Francs.

Collection of British Authors Tauchnitz Edition.

Mrs. Jenkin:
"Who Breaks—Pays" 1 v. Skirmishing 1 v. Once and Again 2 v. Two French Marriages 2 v. Within an Ace 1 v.

Edward Jenkins:
Ginx's Baby; Lord Bantam 2 v.

Douglas Jerrold:
The History of St. Giles and St. James 2 v. Men of Character 2 v.

Johnson:
The Lives of the English Poets 2 v.

Miss Kavanagh:
Nathalie 2 v. Daisy Burns 2 v. Grace Lee 2 v. Rachel Gray 1 v. Adèle 3 v. A Summer and Winter in the Two Sicilies 2 v. Seven Years 2 v. French Women of Letters 1 v. English Women of Letters 1 v. Queen Mab 2 v. Beatrice 2 v. Sybil's Second Love 2 v. Dora 2 v. Silvia 2 v. Bessie 2 v.

R. B. Kimball:
Saint Leger 1 v. Romance of Student Life abroad 1 v. Undercurrents 1 v. Was he Successful? 1 v. To-Day in New-York 1 v.

A. W. Kinglake:
Eothen 1 v. The Invasion of the Crimea v. 1-8.

Charles Kingsley:
Yeast 1 v. Westward ho! 2 v. Two Years ago 2 v. Hypatia 2 v. Alton Locke 1 v. Hereward the Wake 2 v. At Last 2 v.

Henry Kingsley:
Ravenshoe 2 v. Austin Elliot 1 v. The Recollections of Geoffry Hamlyn 2 v. The Hillyars and the Burtons 2 v. Leighton Court 1 v. Valentin 1 v.

Charles Lamb:
The Essays of Elia and Eliana 1 v.

Mary Langdon:
Ida May 1 vol.

"Last of the Cavaliers,"
Author of—
The Last of the Cavaliers 2 v. The Gain of a Loss 2 v.

S. Le Fanu:
Uncle Silas 2 v. Guy Deverell 2 v.

Mark Lemon:
Wait for the End 2 v. Loved at Last 2 v. Falkner Lyle 2 v. Leyton Hall 2 v. Golden Fetters 2 v.

Charles Lever:
The O'Donoghue 1 v. The Knight of Gwynne 3 v. Arthur O'Leary 2 v. The Confessions of Harry Lorrequer 2 v. Charles O'Malley 3 v. Tom Burke of "Ours" 3 v. Jack Hinton 2 v. The Daltons 4 v. The Dodd Family abroad 3 v. The Martins of Cro' Martin 3 v. The Fortunes of Glencore 2 v. Roland Cashel 3 v. Davenport Dunn 3 v. Con Cregan 2 v. One of Them 2 v. Maurice Tiernay 2 v. Sir Jasper Carew 2 v. Barrington 2 v. A Day's Ride: a Life's Romance 2 v. Luttrell of Arran 2 v. Tony Butler 2 v. Sir Brook Fossbrooke 2 v. The Bramleighs of Bishop's Folly 2 v. A Rent in a Cloud 1 v. That Boy of Norcott's 1 v. St. Patrick's Eve; Paul Gosslett's Confessions 1 v. Lord Kilgobbin 2 v.

The price of each volume is ½ Thaler = 2 Francs.

G. H. Lewes:
Ranthorpe 1 v. The Physiology of Common Life 2 v.

Longfellow:
Poetical Works (w. portrait) 3 v. The Divine Comedy of Dante Alighieri 3 v. The New-England Tragedies 1 v. The Divine Tragedy 1 v.

Lutfullah:
Autobiography of Lutfullah, by Eastwick 1 v.

Lord Macaulay:
History of England (w. portrait) 10 v. Critical and Historical Essays 5 v. Lays of Ancient Rome 1 v. Speeches 2 v. Biographical Essays 1 v. William Pitt, Atterbury 1 v.

George MacDonald:
Alec Forbes of Howglen 2 v. Annals of a Quiet Neighbourhood 2 v. David Elginbrod 2 v. The Vicar's Daughter 2 v.

Mrs. Mackarness:
Sunbeam Stories 1 v. A Peerless Wife 2 v. A Mingled Yarn 2 v.

Norman Macleod:
The old Lieutenant and his Son 1 v.

Mrs. Macquoid:
Patty 2 v. Miriam's Marriage 2 v.

"Mademoiselle Mori,"
Author of—
Mademoiselle Mori 2 v. Denise 1 v. Madame Fontenoy 1 v. On the Edge of the Storm 1 v.

Lord Mahon: *vide* Stanhope.

R. Blachford Mansfield:
The Log of the Water Lily 1 v.

Capt. Marryat:
Jacob Faithful (w. portrait) 1 v. Percival Keene 1 v. Peter Simple 1 v. Japhet 1 v. Monsieur Violet 1 v. The Settlers 1 v. The Mission 1 v. The Privateer's-Man 1 v. The Children of the New-Forest 1 v. Valerie 1 v. Mr. Midshipman Easy 1 v. The King's Own 1 v.

Florence Marryat
(Mrs. Ross-Church):
Love's Conflict 2 v. For Ever and Ever 2 v. The Confessions of Gerald Estcourt 2 v. Nelly Brooke 2 v. Véronique 2 v. Petronel 2 v. Her Lord and Master 2 v. The Prey of the Gods 1 v. Life of Captain Marryat 1 v.

Mrs. Marsh:
Ravenscliffe 2 v. Emilia Wyndham 2 v. Castle Avon 2 v. Aubrey 2 v. The Heiress of Haughton 2 v. Evelyn Marston 2 v. The Rose of Ashurst 2 v.

Whyte Melville:
Kate Coventry 1 v. Holmby House 2 v. Digby Grand 1 v. Good for Nothing 2 v. The Queen's Maries 2 v. The Gladiators 2 v. The Brookes of Bridlemere 2 v. Cerise 2 v. The Interpreter 2 v. The White Rose 2 v. M. or N. 1 v. Contraband; or A Losing Hazard 1 v. Sarchedon 2 v.

The price of each volume is ½ Thaler = 2 Francs.

Meredith (Hon. R. Lytton):
Poems 2 v.

Milton:
Poetical Works 1 v.

Miss Florence Montgomery:
Misunderstood 1 v. Thrown Together 2 v.

Moore:
Poetical Works (w. portrait) 5 v.

Lady Morgan's
Memoirs 3 v.

My little Lady 2 v.

New Testament [v. 1000.]

Mrs. Newby:
Common Sense 2 v.

Dr. J. H. Newman:
Callista 1 v.

"No Church," Author of—
No Church 2 v. Owen:—a Waif 2 v.

Hon. Mrs. Norton:
Stuart of Dunleath 2 v. Lost and Saved 2 v. Old Sir Douglas 2 v.

Not Easily Jealous 2 v.

Mrs. Oliphant:
Passages in the Life of Mrs. Margaret Maitland of Sunnyside 1 v. The Last of the Mortimers 2 v. Agnes 2 v. Madonna Mary 2 v. The Minister's Wife 2 v. The Rector, and the Doctor's Family 1 v. Salem Chapel 2 v. The Perpetual Curate 2 v. Miss Marjoribanks 2 v. Ombra 2 v. Memoir of Count de Montalembert 2 v.

Ossian:
Poems 1 v.

Ouida:
Idalia 2 v. Tricotrin 2 v. Puck 2 v. Chandos 2 v. Strathmore 2 v. Under two Flags 2 v. Folle-Farine 2 v. A Leaf in the Storm; A Dog of Flanders & other Stories 1 v. Cecil Castlemaine's Gage 1 v. Madame la Marquise 1 v.

Miss Parr
(Holme Lee):
Basil Godfrey's Caprice 2 v. For Richer, for Poorer 2 v. The Beautiful Miss Barrington 2 v. Her Title of Honour 1 v. Echoes of a Famous Year 1 v.

Mrs. Parr:
Dorothy Fox 1 v.

"Paul Ferroll," Author of—
Paul Ferroll 1 v. Year after Year 1 v. Why Paul Ferroll killed his Wife 1 v.

Miss Fr. M. Peard:
One Year 2 v. The Rose-Garden 1 v. Unawares 1 v.

Bishop Percy:
Reliques of Ancient English Poetry 3 v.

Pope:
Select Poetical Works (w. portrait) 1 v.

The Prince Consort's
Speeches and Addresses 1 v.

The price of each volume is ½ Thaler = 2 Francs.

Charles Reade:
"It is never too late to mend" 2 v. "Love me little, love me long" 1 v. The Cloister and the Hearth 2 v. Hard Cash 3 v. Put Yourself in his Place 2 v. A Terrible Temptation 2 v. Peg Woffington 1 v.

Recommended to Mercy:
Author of—
Recommended to Mercy 2 v. Zoe's 'Brand' 2 v.

Richardson:
Clarissa Harlowe 4 v.

Rev. W. Robertson:
Sermons 4 v.

Charles H. Ross:
The Pretty Widow 1 v. A London Romance 2 v.

J. Ruffini:
Lavinia 2 v. Doctor Antonio 1 v. Lorenzo Benoni 1 v. Vincenzo 2 v. A Quiet Nook 1 v. The Paragreens on a Visit to Paris 1 v. Carlino and other Stories 1 v.

G. A. Sala:
The Seven Sons of Mammon 2 v.

Katherine Saunders:
Joan Merryweather and other Tales 1 v.

Sir Walter Scott:
Waverley (w. portrait) 1 v. The Antiquary 1 v. Ivanhoe 1 v. Kenilworth 1 v. Quentin Durward 1 v. Old Mortality 1 v. Guy Mannering 1 v. Rob Roy 1 v. The Pirate 1 v. The Fortunes of Nigel 1 v. The Black Dwarf; A Legend of Montrose 1 v. The Bride of Lammermoor 1 v. The Heart of Mid-Lothian 2 v. The Monastery 1 v. The Abbot 1 v. Peveril of the Peak 2 v. The Poetical Works 2 v. Woodstock 1 v. The Fair Maid of Perth 1 v. Anne of Geierstein 1 v.

Miss Sewell:
Amy Herbert 2 v. Ursula 2 v. A Glimpse of the World 2 v. The Journal of a Home Life 2 v. After Life 2 v.

Shakespeare:
Plays and Poems (w. portrait) compl. 7 v. *(Second Edition.)*
Shakespeare's Plays may also be had in 37 numbers, at $^1/_{10}$ Thlr. each number.
Doubtful Plays 1 v.

Shelley:
A Selection from his Poems 1 v.

Nathan Sheppard:
Shut up in Paris 1 v.

Sheridan:
Dramatic Works 1 v.

Smollett:
The Adventures of Roderick Random 1 v. The Expedition of Humphry Clinker 1 v. The Adventures of Peregrine Pickle 2 v.

Earl Stanhope:
History of England 7 v. The Reign of Queen Anne 2 v.

The price of each volume is ½ Thaler = 2 Francs.

Sterne:
The Life and Opinions of Tristram Shandy 1 v. A Sentimental Journey 1 v.

"Still Waters," Author of—
Still Waters 1 v. Dorothy 1 v. De Cressy 1 v. Uncle Ralph 1 v. Maiden Sisters 1 v. Martha Brown 1 v.

Mrs. H. Beecher Stowe:
Uncle Tom's Cabin (w. portrait) 2 v. A Key to Uncle Tom's Cabin 2 v. Dred 2 v. The Minister's Wooing 1 v. Oldtown Folks 2 v.

Swift:
Gulliver's Travels 1 v.

Baroness Tautphoeus:
Cyrilla 2 v. The Initials 2 v. Quits 2 v. At Odds 2 v.

Colonel Meadows Taylor:
Tara: a Mahratta Tale 3 v.

H. Templeton:
Diary and Notes 1 v.

Tennyson:
Poetical Works 7 v.

W. M. Thackeray:
Vanity Fair 3 v. The History of Pendennis 3 v. Miscellanies 8 v. The History of Henry Esmond 2 v. The English Humourists 1 v. The Newcomes 4 v. The Virginians 4 v. The Four Georges; Lovel the Widower 1 v. The Adventures of Philip 2 v. Denis Duval 1 v. Roundabout Papers 2 v. Catherine 1 v. The Irish Sketch-Book 2 v.

Miss Thackeray:
The Story of Elizabeth 1 v. The Village on the Cliff 1 v.

A. Thomas:
Denis Donne 2 v. On Guard 2 v. Walter Goring 2 v. Played out 2 v. Called to Account 2 v. Only Herself 2 v.

Thomson:
Poetical Works (w. portrait) 1 v.

F. G. Trafford (Mrs. Riddell):
George Geith of Fen Court 2 v. Maxwell Drewitt 2 v. The Race for Wealth 2 v. Far above Rubies 2 v.

Trois-Etoiles:
The Member for Paris 2 v.

Anthony Trollope:
Doctor Thorne 2 v. The Bertrams 2 v. The Warden 1 v. Barchester Towers 2 v. Castle Richmond 2 v. The West Indies 1 v. Framley Parsonage 2 v. North America 3 v. Orley Farm 3 v. Rachel Ray 2 v. The Small House at Allington 3 v. Can you forgive her? 3 v. The Belton Estate 2 v. The Last Chronicle of Barset 3 v. The Claverings 2 v. Phineas Finn 3 v. He knew he was Right 3 v. The Vicar of Bullhampton 2 v. Sir Harry Hotspur of Humblethwaite 1 v. Ralph the Heir 2 v. The Golden Lion of Granpere 1 v.

T. Adolphus Trollope:
The Garstangs of Garstang Grange 2 v. A Siren 2 v.

The price of each volume is ½ Thaler = 2 Francs.

The Two Cosmos 1 v.

"Véra,"
Author of—
Véra 1 v. The Hôtel du Petit St. Jean 1 v.

Eliot Warburton:
The Crescent and the Cross 2 v. Darien 2 v.

S. Warren:
Passages from the Diary of a late Physician 2 v. Ten Thousand a-Year 3 v. Now and Then 1 v. The Lily and the Bee 1 v.

Waterdale Neighbours 2 v.

Miss Wetherell:
The wide, wide World 1 v. Queechy 2 v. The Hills of the Shatemuc 2 v. Say and Seal 2 v. The Old Helmet 2 v.

A Whim
and its Consequences 1 v.

Mrs. Henry Wood:
East Lynne 3 v. The Channings 2 v. Mrs. Halliburton's Troubles 2 v. Verner's Pride 3 v. The Shadow of Ashlydyat 3 v. Trevlyn Hold 2 v. Lord Oakburn's Daughters 2 v. Oswald Cray 2 v. Mildred Arkell 2 v. St. Martin's Eve 2 v. Elster's Folly 2 v. Lady Adelaide's Oath 2 v. Orville College 1 v. A Life's Secret 1 v. The Red Court Farm 2 v. Anne Hereford 2 v. Roland Yorke 2 v. George Canterbury's Will 2 v. Bessy Rane 2 v. Dene Hollow 2 v. The Foggy Night at Offord etc. 1 v. Within the Maze 2 v.

Wordsworth:
Select Poetical Works 2 v.

Lascelles Wraxall:
Wild Oats 1 v.

Edm. Yates:
Land at Last 2 v. Broken to Harness 2 v. The Forlorn Hope 2 v. Black Sheep 2 v. The Rock Ahead 2 v. Wrecked in Port 2 v. Dr. Wainwright's Patient 2 v. Nobody's Fortune 2 v. Castaway 2 v. A Waiting Race 2 v. The Yellow Flag 2 v.

Miss Yonge:
The Heir of Redclyffe 2 v. Heartsease 2 v. The Daisy Chain 2 v. Dynevor Terrace 2 v. Hopes and Fears 2 v. The Young Step-Mother 2 v. The Trial 2 v. The Clever Woman of the Family 2 v. The Dove in the Eagle's Nest 2 v. The Danvers Papers; the Prince and the Page 1 v. The Chaplet of Pearls 2 v. The two Guardians 1 v. The Caged Lion 2 v.

The price of each volume is ½ Thaler = 2 Francs.

Series for the Young.

Kenneth; or, the Rear-Guard of the Grand Army. By *Miss Yonge* (Author of "the Heir of Redclyffe"). With Frontispiece, 1 v.

Ruth and her Friends. A Story for Girls. With Frontispiece, 1 v.

Our Year: A Child's Book, in Prose and Verse. By the Author of "John Halifax, Gentleman." Illustrated by Clarence Dobell, 1 v.

Ministering Children. A Tale dedicated to Childhood. By *Maria Louisa Charlesworth*. With Frontispiece, 1 v.

The Little Duke. Ben Sylvester's Word. By *Miss Yonge* (Author of "the Heir of Redclyffe"). With a Frontispiece by B. Plockhorst, 1 v.

The Stokesley Secret. By *Miss Yonge* (Author of "the Heir of Redclyffe"). With a Frontispiece by B. Plockhorst, 1 v.

Tales from Shakspeare. By *Charles* and *Mary Lamb*. With the Portrait of Shakspeare 1 v.

Countess Kate. By *Miss Yonge* (Author of "the Heir of Redclyffe"). With Frontispiece, 1 v.

Three Tales for Boys. By the Author of "John Halifax, Gentleman." With a Frontispiece by B. Plockhorst, 1 v.

A Book of Golden Deeds. By *Miss Yonge* (Author of "the Heir of Redclyffe"). With a Frontispiece by B. Plockhorst, 2 v.

Moral Tales. By *Maria Edgeworth*. With a Frontispiece by B. Plockhorst, 1 v.

Friarswood Post-Office. By *Miss Yonge* (Author of "the Heir of Redclyffe"). With Frontispiece, 1 v.

Cousin Trix and her welcome Tales. By *Miss Georgiana Craik*. With a Frontispiece by B. Plockhorst, 1 v.

Three Tales for Girls. By the Author of "John Halifax, Gentleman." With a Frontispiece by B. Plockhorst, 1 v.

Henrietta's Wish; or, Domineering. A Tale. By *Miss Yonge* (Author of "the Heir of Redclyffe"). With a Frontispiece by B. Plockhorst, 1 v.

Kings of England: A History for the Young. By *Miss Yonge* (Author of "the Heir of Redclyffe"). With Frontispiece, 1 v.

Popular Tales. By *Maria Edgeworth*. With a Frontispiece by B. Plockhorst, 2 v.

The Lances of Lynwood; the Pigeon Pie. By *Miss Yonge* (Author of "the Heir of Redclyffe"). With Frontispiece, 1 v.

The price of each volume is ½ Thaler = 2 Francs.

Collection of German Authors.

On the Heights. By *B. Auerbach*. Translated by F. E. Bunnett. Second Authorized Edition, thoroughly revised. 3 v.

In the Year '13: By *Fritz Reuter*. Translated from the Platt-Deutsch by Charles Lee Lewes, 1 v.

Faust. By *Goethe*. From the German by John Anster, LL.D. 1 v.

Undine, Sintram and other Tales. By *Fouqué*. Translated by F. E. Bunnett, 1 v.

L'Arrabiata and other Tales. By *Paul Heyse*. From the German by M. Wilson, 1 v.

The Princess of Brunswick-Wolfenbüttel and other Tales. By *H. Zschokke*. From the German by M. A. Faber, 1 v.

Nathan the Wise and Emilia Galotti. By *G. E. Lessing*. The former translated by W. Taylor, the latter by Charles Lee Lewes, 1 v.

Behind the Counter [Handel und Wandel]. By *F. W. Hackländer*. From the German by Mary Howitt, 1 v.

Three Tales by *W. Hauff*. From the German by M. A. Faber, 1 v.

Joachim von Kamern and Diary of a poor young Lady. By *Maria Nathusius*. From the German by Miss Thompson, 1 v.

Poems from the German of *Ferdinand Freiligrath*. Edited by his Daughter. Second Copyright Edition, enlarged. 1 v.

Gabriel. A Story of the Jews in Prague. By *S. Kohn*. From the German by Arthur Milman, M.A., 1 v.

The Dead Lake and other Tales. By *Paul Heyse*. From the German by Mary Wilson. 1 v.

Through Night to Light. By *Karl Gutzkow*. From the German by M. A. Faber, 1 v.

An Egyptian Princess. By *Georg Ebers*. Translated by E. Grove, 2 v.

Flower, Fruit and Thorn Pieces: or the Married Life, Death, and Wedding of the Advocate of the Poor, Firmian Stanislaus Siebenkäs. By *Jean Paul Friederich Richter*. Translated from the German by E. H. Noel, 2 v.

Ekkehard. A Tale of the tenth Century. By *J. V. Scheffel*. Translated from the German by Sofie Delffs, 2 v.

The Princess of the Moor [das Haideprinzesschen]. By *E. Marlitt*, 2 v.

The price of each volume is ½ Thaler = 2 Francs.

Dictionaries.

Dictionary of the English and German languages for general use. Compiled with especial regard to the elucidation of modern literature, the Pronunciation and Accentuation after the principles of Walker and Heinsius. By *W. James.* Twenty-third Stereotype Edition, *thoroughly revised and greatly enlarged.* 8vo sewed 1½ Thlr.

Dictionary of the English and French languages for general use with the Accentuation and a literal Pronunciation of every word in both languages. Compiled from the best and most approved English and French authorities. By *W. James* and *A. Moll.* Eleventh Stereotype Edition. 8vo sewed 2 Thlr.

Dictionary of the English and Italian languages for general use with the Italian Pronunciation and the Accentuation of every word in both languages and the terms of Science and Art, of Mechanics, Railways, Marine &c. Compiled from the best and most recent English and Italian Dictionaries. By *W. James* and *Gius. Grassi.* Seventh Stereotype Edition. 8vo sewed 1¾ Thlr.

New Pocket Dictionary of the English and German languages. By *J. E. Wessely.* Fourth Stereotype Edition. 16mo sewed ½ Thlr. bound ¾ Thlr.

New Pocket Dictionary of the English and French languages. By *J. E. Wessely.* Fifth Stereotype Edition. 16mo sewed ½ Thlr. bound ¾ Thlr.

New Pocket Dictionary of the English and Italian languages. By *J. E. Wessely.* Second Stereotype Edition. 16mo sewed ½ Thlr. bound ¾ Thlr.

New Pocket Dictionary of the English and Spanish languages. By *J. E. Wessely* and *A. Gironés.* Second Stereotype Edition. 16mo sewed ½ Thlr. bound ¾ Thlr.

www.ingramcontent.com/pod-product-compliance
Lightning Source LLC
Chambersburg PA
CBHW031331230426
43670CB00006B/310